The Dennis Wheatley Library of the Occult
Volume 21

Satanism and Witches is a collection of
essays and stories which date from the
sixteenth century to the present day. There
are historical records of the notorious Salem
Witch Trials and accounts of the practice of
Black Magic today – a very varied selection
which provides much interesting and valuable
information on the supernatural.

The Dennis Wheatley Library of the Occult

Satanism and Witches

Essays and stories selected by
DENNIS WHEATLEY

SPHERE BOOKS LIMITED
30/32 Gray's Inn Road, London WC1X 8JL

First published in Great Britain by Sphere Books Ltd 1974
Introduction copyright © Dennis Wheatley 1974
Anthology copyright © Sphere Books Ltd 1974

TRADE
MARK

Set in Intertype Baskerville

Printed in Great Britain by
Hazell Watson & Viney Ltd
Aylesbury, Bucks

ISBN 0 7221 9038 7

ACKNOWLEDGMENTS

The publishers would like to thank the following for permission to include copyright material in this collection:
Mrs Elizabeth Sax Rohmer and Associated Book Publishers for 'The Witch Finders' from *The Romance of Sorcery*; to Robert Graves for 'Modern Witchcraft' from *The Crane Bag*; to John Symonds for 'The Black Lodge'; to Duckworth & Co Ltd and Betty May for 'The Sacrifice' from *Tiger Woman*; to Faber & Faber Ltd for 'The Initiation to Witchcraft' from *The God of the Witches*; to Hutchinson & Co Ltd for 'Sylvan Horrors' and 'Vampires, Were-Wolves, Fox-Women, Etc'.
Every effort has been made to find the owners of the copyrighted stories, but if necessary acknowledgments have been omitted, or any stories included without due permission, we trust the copyright-holders will accept our apologies.

CONTENTS

Six articles   Dennis Wheatley

INTRODUCTION

This is an out-of-series volume; for it is neither a novel, a serious study of some aspect of the occult nor a collection of short stories. It is a book mainly of essays that contain so much valuable information upon supernatural happenings, and historical records of witchcraft, that I feel it would be a serious omission not to include them in this Library.

The earliest of them dates back to the mid-1500s and is by that remarkable genius Benvenuto Cellini. He was a man of many interests and here tells us of his attempt to raise the spirit of his dead mistress, Angelica.

Sax Rohmer gives us an account of the horrifying fate that overtook scores of people in Europe who were accused of witchcraft during the following two hundred years, the tortures they suffered and the iniquities of professional witch-finders such as Matthew Hopkins.

During the seventeenth century witch-baiting was at its height. In Britain it was initiated by King James I in 1597 and William Godwin writes of the Lancashire Witches, who were the subject of Harrison Ainsworth's famous novel. In Germany witchcraft was particularly prevalent and Robert Anthony gives us a graphic picture of its practice there.

In the 1670s and 1680s Paris was riddled with practitioners of the black art. This led to the 'Chambre Ardente Affair' about which Ronald Seth tells us. Francis Mossiker's long novel *The Affair of the Poisons* also deals with this and contains a detailed description of the infamous Abbé Gibourg performing the Black Mass on Madame de Montespan. We are publishing it in our Library in February 1975.

With her *The Initiation to Witchcraft* Professor Margaret Murray, famous for her books, *The Witch Cult in Western Europe* and *The God of the Witches*, gives us a graphic description of the abominable ceremonies by which Satan accepted his devotees and conferred occult powers on them. And P. T. Barnum writes on the questionable effect of casting spells.

At the end of the seventeenth century there occurred the terrible scandal of the Witch Trials in Salem, when nearly everyone in the town became possessed. Cotton Mather, a puritanical Boston minister, writes here about the trials. Then a hundred years later Nathaniel Hawthorne – the father of American Literature – who was born in Salem, gives us a story describing the Salem Mass.

With Aleister Crowley's episode (although not admitted) from his own autobiography we come to comparatively modern times, and learn of 'The Black Lodge'. This is followed by Betty May's account of life at the Abbey Thelame on the island of Cefalú, to which she went only reluctantly, because her husband was one of Crowley's disciples.

Elliott O'Donnell, a master of occult literature, tells us of strange happenings. And that great writer, Robert Graves, describes a revival of witch-hunting in Germany under the Nazis.

There are in addition five anonymous pieces – 'An Indictment for Witchcraft', 'A Pact with the Devil', 'How to Raise a Spirit', 'The Black Goat of Brandenburg' and 'The Confession of the Witches of Elfdale'.

Also six essays by myself concerning witches, sabbats, and the black art, that I wrote for a national paper some years ago.

Finally we give 'The Secret Grimoire of Turiel' which portends to tell one how to raise a demon. But if you try it and fail, please don't ask me for your money back.

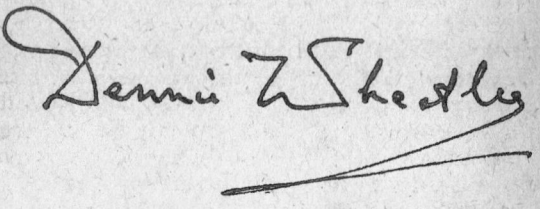

MY EXPERIENCES IN NECROMANCY

Benvenuto Cellini

It happened, through a variety of odd accidents, that I made acquaintance with a Sicilian priest, who was a man of genius, and well versed in the Latin and Greek authors. Happening one day to have some conversation with him, when the subject turned on the subject of necromancy, I, who had a great desire to know something of the matter, told him, that I had all my life felt a curiosity to be acquainted with the mysteries of this art. The priest made answer, 'That the man must be of a resolute and steady temper who enters upon that study.' I replied, 'That I had fortitude and resolution enough, if I could but find an opportunity.' The priest subjoined, 'If you think you have the heart to venture, I will give you all the satisfaction you can desire.' Thus we agreed to enter upon a plan of necromancy. The priest one evening prepared to satisfy me, and desired me to look out for a companion or two. I invited one Vincenzio Romoli, who was my intimate acquaintance : he brought with him a native of Pistoia, who cultivated the black art himself. We repaired to the Colloseo, and the priest, according to the custom of necromancers, began to draw circles upon the ground with the most impressive ceremonies imaginable : he likewise brought hither assafoetida, several precious perfumes and fire, with some compositions also which diffused noisome odours. As soon as he was in readiness, he made an opening to the circle, and having taken us by the hand, ordered the other necromancer, his partner, to throw the perfumes into the fire at the proper time, entrusting the care of the fire and the perfumes to the rest; and then he began his incantations. This ceremony lasted above an hour and a half, when there appeared several legions of devils insomuch that the amphitheatre was quite filled with them. I was busy about the perfumes, when the priest, perceiving there was a considerable number of infernal spirits, turned to me and said, '*Benvenuto*, ask them something,' I answered, 'Let them bring me into the company of my Sicilian mistress, Angelica.' That night we obtained no answer of any sort; but I had received great satisfaction in having my curiosity so far indulged. The necromancer told me, it was requisite we should go a second time, assuring me, that I should be satisfied in whatever I asked; but that I must bring with me a pure immaculate boy.

I took with me a youth who was in my service, of about twelve years of age, together with the same Vincenzio Romoli, who had been my companion the first time and one Agnolino Gaddi, an intimate acquaintance, whom I likewise prevailed on to assist at the ceremony. When we came to the place appointed, the priest having made his preparations as before, with the same and even more striking ceremonies, placed us within the circle, which he had likewise drawn with a more wonderful art, and in a more solemn manner, than at our former meeting. Thus having committed the care of the perfume and the fire to my friend Vincenzio, who was assisted by Agnolino Gaddi, he put into my hand a pintacula or magical chart, and bid me turn it towards the place that he should direct me and under the pintacula I held the boy. The necromancer having begun to make his tremendous invocations, called by their names a multitude of demons, who were the leaders of the several legions, and questioned them by the power of the eternal uncreated God, who lives for ever, in the Hebrew language, as likewise in Latin and Greek : insomuch that the amphitheatre was almost in an instant filled with demons more numerous than at the former conjuration. Vincenzio Romoli was busied in making a fire, with the assistance of Agnolino, and burning a great quantity of precious perfumes. I, by the direction of the necromancer, again desired to be in the company of my Angelica. The former thereupon turning to me, said, 'Know, they have declared, that in the space of a month you shall be in her company.'

He then requested me to stand resolutely by him, because the legions were now above a thousand more in number than he had designed; and, besides these were the most dangerous; so that, after they had answered my question, it behoved him to be civil to them, and dismiss them quietly. At the same time the boy under the pintacula was in a terrible fright, saying, that there were in that place a million of fierce men, who threatened to destroy us; and that, more-over, four armed giants of an enormous stature were endeavouring to break into our circle. During this time, whilst the necromancer, trembling with fear, endeavoured by mild and gentle methods to dismiss them in the best way he could, Vincenzio Romoli, who quivered like an aspen leaf, took care of the perfumes. Though I was as much terrified as any of them, I did my utmost to conceal the terror I felt; so that I greatly contributed to inspire the rest with resolution; but the truth is, I gave myself over for a dead man, seeing the horrid fright the necromancer was in. The boy placed his head between his knees, and said, 'In this posture I will die; for we shall all surely perish.' I told him that all these demons were under us, and what he saw was smoke and shadow; so I bid him hold up his head and take courage. No sooner did he look up, but he cried out, 'The whole amphitheatre is burning, and the fire is just falling upon us,' so covering his eyes with his hands, he again exclaimed that destruction was inevitable, and he desired to see no more. The necromancer entreated me to have a good heart, and take care to burn the proper perfumes; upon which I turned to Romoli, and bid him burn all the most precious perfumes he had. At the same time I cast my eye upon Agnolino Gaddi, who was terrified to such a degree that he could scarce distinguish objects, and seemed to be half-dead. Seeing him in this condition, I said. 'Agnolino, upon these occasions a man should not yield to fear, but should stir about and give his assistance; so come directly and put on some more of these perfumes.' Poor Agnolino, upon attempting to move, was so violently terrified that the effects of his fear overpowered all the perfumes we were burning. The boy, hearing a crepitation, ventured once more to raise his head, when, seeing me laugh, he began to take courage, and said, 'That the devils were flying away with a vengeance.'

In this condition we stayed till the bell rang for morning prayer. The boy again told us, that there remained but few devils, and these were at a great distance. When the magician had performed the rest of his ceremonies, he stripped off his gown and took up a wallet full of books which he had brought with him. We all went out of the circle together, keeping as close to each other as we possibly could, especially the boy, who had placed himself in the middle, holding the necromancer by the coat, and me by the cloak. As we were going to our houses in the quarter of Banchi, the boy told us that two of the demons whom we had seen at the amphitheatre, went on before us leaping and skipping, sometimes running upon the roofs of the houses, and sometimes upon the ground. The priest declared, that though he had often entered magic circles nothing so extraordinary had ever happened to him. As we went along, he would fain persuade me to assist with him at consecrating a book, from which, he said, we should derive immense riches : we should then ask the demons to discover to us the various treasures with which the earth abounds, which would raise us to opulence and power; but that those love-affairs were mere follies, from whence no good could be expected. I answered, 'That I would readily have accepted his proposal if I understood Latin', he redoubled his persuasions, assuring me, that the knowledge of the Latin language was by no means material. He added, that he could have Latin scholars enough, if he had thought it worth while to look out for them; but that he could never have met with a partner of resolution and intrepidity equal to mine, and that I should by all means follow his advice. Whilst we were engaged in this conversation, we arrived at our respective homes, and all that night dreamt of nothing but devils.

I assisted him at another evocation a few days afterwards. I was overjoyed when the promise, previously made, of beholding my beloved mistress, Angelica, for the space of several minutes, materialised.

THE WITCH FINDERS

Sax Rohmer

With the increase of the sorcery epidemic uprose a class of persons whose business was the seeking out and burning of witches and sorcerers. Sprenger, in Germany, has the dubious honour of being the most active of these. He has laid down a regular form of trial, together with a course of examination by which his colleagues in other countries might discover the brand of Lucifer.

This individual alone made himself responsible for some 500 victims annually! Within three months, 900 perished in Würzburg, 600 in Bamberg, and 500 in Geneva. One judge of Lorraine boasted that he had personally condemned 900; and the Archbishop of Trèves, ascribing the cold spring of 1586 to witchcraft burned 118 women at one time.

'Pricking' was the favourite mode employed by the witch-finder to learn if the suspected person were one of Satan's own, and the discharge of fourteen alleged witches by the Parliament of Paris, in 1589, appears to be the only notable instance of mercy throughout the whole black record. On this occasion, four commissioners – Pierre Pigray, the King's surgeon, and Messrs. Leroi, Renard, and Falaiseau, the King's physicians – were appointed to examine these witches in quest of the devil's mark.

Pierre Pigray relates that the examination took place in the presence of two Court Counsellors. The witches were all stripped naked, and the physicians examined their bodies with great care, 'pricking' them in all the marks they could find to learn if these were insensible to pain – a certain proof of guilt.

The poor women, however, were very sensible of the pricking, screaming when the pins were driven into them. 'Many of them were quite indifferent about life, and one or two desired death as a relief from their sufferings.' They were released, however.

A French theological Professor, who wrote in 1720, notes the following symptoms as being infallible signs of a person having been bewitched :

1. The vomiting of needles, nails, and pieces of glass.
2. Continual burning and lancinating pains, especially in the region of the heart, inability to retain food, and a sensation as if balls were rising and falling in the throat.
3. Suddenly falling ill of a grievous complaint, and wasting away without any apparent cause.
4. Medicines prescribed having the opposite effect from their known virtues and intensifying rather than modifying the disease.

To such an absurd extent were the proceedings against witches carried on the Continent, that it is related how, on one occasion, a sow and a litter of pigs were prosecuted. The whole family was found guilty and condemned to death; but the infant porkers were reprieved on account of their youth!

The following is transcribed from an old chap-book which had a wide circulation in the seventeenth century :

'To help a Person under an ill Tongue, and make the Witch appear, or the Effect cease.

'Cut off some of the Party's Hair, just at the Nape of the Neck, clip it small and burn it to Powder, put the Powder in Sal-Armoniack, write the Party's Name you suspect backwards, and put the Paper, dipt in *Aqua Vitœ,* into the other two, then set it over a gentle Fire; let the Party afflicted sit by it, and diligently watch it that it run not over to catch flame, speaking no Word, whatsoever Noise is heard, but take Notice of what Voice or Roaring is heard in the Chimney, or any part of the Room, and then write how often you hear it, and fix before each writing this Character, ☽ – and if the Party who afflicts you appear not Visible, though you may know the Voice, repeat it again, and if she appear in no visible shape, it may make her charm impotent, and give relief to the Afflicted Party.'

Famous among witch-finders was James VI of Scotland; and, if his work on demonology has not rendered him immortal, by reason of his dealings with those suspected of witchcraft at least he is for ever execrable. The torturing of the young and handsome Gellie Duncan, and the infamous torments to which her reputed accomplice, Cunningham (Dr. Fian), was submitted, are but some of the items to the debit of James VI of Scotland.

Dr. Fian was far removed from a saintly character but

when his examination by James was concluded (restoratives having been administered again and again in order to render the victim conscious of renewed tortures) he was less a man than a bleeding mass, for even the bones of his legs had been crushed to pulp in the boot; his nails had been withdrawn by pincers and needles thrust into his eyes to the sockets.

Euphemia Macalzean (another alleged accomplice of poor Gellie Duncan) was doomed 'to be burned in ashes, *quick* [alive] to the death'. This inhuman sentence was carried out on June 25, 1591.

In 1597 James published in Edinburgh his treatise on demonology. In the introduction he says :

'The fearful abounding at this time and in this country of these detestable slaves of the devil, the witches or enchanters, hath moved me, beloved reader, to dispatch in post this following treatise of mine, not in any wise, as I protest, to serve for a show of mine own learning and ingene, but only (moved of conscience) to press thereby . . . that the instrument . . . merits most severely to be punished, against the damnable opinions of two, principally in our age; whereof the one called Scot, an Englishman, is not ashamed in public print to deny that there can be such things as witchcraft . . .'

Other parts of his work James thoughtfully cast in the form of dialogue, to render it, in his own words, 'more pleasant and facile' !

England and Scotland, then, soon competed with the Continental countries in the burning of witches, and Zachary Grey, the editor of *Hadibras*, says that he himself perused a list of three thousand victims executed during the session of the Long Parliament alone. 1634 is notorious for the trial of the 'Lancashire Witches', but it remained for Manningtree, Essex, about the year 1644, to present to the world a master witch-finder, in the vulgar person of Matthew Hopkins. Assuming the title of 'Witch-finder General', Hopkins toured the counties of Norfolk, Essex, Hants, and Sussex, in quest of witches. In one year he brought no fewer than sixty to the stake.

The method of detection upon which he pinned his faith was that of 'swimming' – so highly recommended by James VI of Scotland. The right thumb of the suspected person was tied to the toe of the left foot, and *vice versa*. She was then wrapped in a blanket and placed on her back in a pond. If she floated – which we are told was generally the case when placed carefully upon the water – she was guilty, and was burned forthwith; if she sank, she was innocent!

Hopkins travelled like a gentleman, attended by his two assistants, always putting up at the principal inn of the town – at the cost of the authorities. He charged 20s. per visit, with expenses, and 20s. per head for each witch convicted.

He had carried on his outrageous trade for three years when the Rev. Mr. Gaul, of Houghton, published a pamphlet directed against the cruel rogue. In it he describes another method employed by Hopkins to detect a witch. He relates that the Witch-finder General used to place the suspected woman in the middle of a room, cross-legged upon a stool. Hopkins then caused her to be watched by his assistants for four-and-twenty hours, during which time she was kept without food or drink.

The interesting theory was that one of her imps would come during that time to suck her blood. As the imp might come in the form of a fly, of a wasp, or of any other insect, and as doors and windows were thoughtfully left open, visitations by imps were common under the circumstances. It was the duty of the watchers to kill any insect which appeared; if a fly escaped, it was her imp – the woman was guilty, she was sentenced to the stake, and Matthew Hopkins collected his modest fee of 20s. from the local authorities.

Of Matthew Hopkins Butler says in *Hudibras*:

> *Hath not this present Parliament*
> *A lieger to the devil sent,*
> *Fully empowered to treat about*
> *Finding revolted witches out?*
> *And has he not within a year*
> *Hang'd threescore of them in one shire?*
> *Some only for not being drown'd,*
> *And some for sitting above ground*
> *Whole days and nights upon their breeches,*
> *And feeling pain, were hang'd for witches;*
> *And some for putting knavish tricks*
> *Upon green geese or turkey chicks;*
> *Or pigs that suddenly deceased*
> *Of griefs unnatural, as he guessed;*
> *Who proved himself at length a witch,*
> *And made a rod for his own breech.*

One rejoices to learn that Matthew Hopkins was 'swum', according to his own recipe, in a Suffolk village-pond, and either drowned or was subsequently executed.

In Scotland, at this period, witch-finders flourished under the generic title of 'common prickers', receiving, like the talented Hopkins, a fee for each conviction. John Kincaid, the common pricker of Dalkeith, in 1646, was caused by the magistrates to exercise his craft upon the person of one Janet Peaston.

'He found two marks of the devil's making,' says Pitcairn, in *Records of Justiciary*, 'for she could not feel the pin when it was put into either of the said marks . . . they were pins of three inches in length.' !

Hundreds of innocent persons had suffered at the hands of the common prickers ere, in 1678, the Privy Council of Scotland sat to consider the appeal of an honest woman who had been indecently exposed by one of them, and expressed the opinion that 'common prickers were *common cheats*'.

THE LANCASHIRE WITCHES

William Godwin

A more melancholy tale does not occur in the annals of
necromancy than that of the Lancashire witches in 1612.
The scene of this story is in Pendlebury Forest, four or five
miles from Manchester, remarkable for its picturesque and
gloomy situation. Such places were not sought then as now,
that they might afford food for the imagination, and gratify
the refined taste of the traveller. They were rather shunned
as infamous for scenes of depredation and murder, or as the
consecrated haunts of diabolical intercourse. Pendlebury
had been long of ill repute on this latter account, when a
country magistrate, Roger Nowel by name, conceived about
this time that he should do a public service, by rooting out a
nest of witches, who rendered the place a terror to all the
neighbouring people. The first persons he seized on were
Elizabeth Demdike and Ann Chattox, the former of whom
was eighty years of age, and had for some years been blind,
who subsisted principally by begging, though she had a
miserable hovel on the spot, which she called her own. Ann
Chattox was of the same age, and had for some time been
threatened with the calamity of blindness. Demdike was held
to be so hardened a witch, that she had trained all her family
to the mystery; namely, Elizabeth Device, her daughter, and
James and Alison Device, her grandchildren. In the accusation of Chattox was also involved Ann Redferne, her
daughter. These, together with John Bulcock, and Jane his
mother, Alice Nutter, Catherine Hewit, and Isabel Roby,
were successively apprehended by the diligence of Nowel
and one or two neighbouring magistrates, and were all of
them by some means induced, some to make a more liberal,
and others a more restricted confession of their misdeeds in
witchcraft, and were afterwards hurried away to Lancaster
Castle, fifty miles off, to prison. Their crimes were said to
have universally proceeded from malignity and resentment;
and it was reported to have repeatedly happened for poor
old Demdike to be led by night from her habitation into the
open air by some member of her family, when she was left

alone for an hour to curse her victim, and pursue her unholy incantations, and was then sought, and brought again to her hovel. Her curses never failed to produce the desired effect.

These poor wretches had been but a short time in prison, when information was given, that a meeting of witches was held on Good Friday, at Malkin's Tower, the habitation of Elizabeth Device, to the number of twenty persons, to consult how by infernal machinations to kill one Covel, an officer, to blow up Lancaster Castle, and deliver the prisoners, and to kill another man of the name of Lister. The last was effected. The other plans by some means, we are not told how, were prevented.

The prisoners were kept in jail till the summer assizes; and in the mean time it fortunately happened that the poor blind Demdike died in confinement, and was never brought up to trial.

The other prisoners were severally indicted for killing by witchcraft certain persons who were named, and were all found guilty. The principal witnesses against Elizabeth Device were James Device and Jennet Device, her grandchildren, the latter only nine years of age. When this girl was put into the witness-box, the grandmother, on seeing her, set up so dreadful a yell, intermixed with bitter curses that the child declared that she could not go on with her evidence, unless the prisoner was removed. This was agreed to; and both brother and sister swore that they had been present when the devil came to their grandmother in the shape of a black dog, and asked her what she desired. She said, the death of John Robinson; when the dog told her to make an image of Robinson in clay, and after crumble it into dust, and as fast as the image perished, the life of the victim should waste away, and in conclusion the man should die. This evidence was received; and upon such testimony, and testimony like this, ten persons were led to the gallows, on the twentieth of August, Ann Chattox of eighty years of age among the rest, the day after the trials, which lasted two days, were finished. The judges who presided on these trials were Sir James Altham and Sir Edward Bromley, barons of the exchequer.*

From the whole of this story it is fair to infer, that these old women had played at the game of commerce with the devil. It had flattered their vanity, to make their simpler

* *Discovery of the Witches*, 1612, printed by order of the Court.

neighbours afraid of them. To observe the symptoms of their rustic terror, even of their hatred and detestation, had been gratifying to them. They played the game so long, that in an imperfect degree they deceived themselves. Human passions are always to a certain degree infectious. Perceiving the hatred of their neighbours, they began to think that they were worthy objects of detestation and terror, that their imprecations had a real effect, and their curses killed. The brown horrors of the forest were favourable to visions; and they sometimes almost believed that they met with the foe of mankind in the night. But, when Elizabeth Device actually saw her grandchild of nine years old placed in the witness-box, with the intention of consigning her to a public and an ingnominious end, then the reveries of the imagination vanished, and she deeply felt the reality, that, where she had been somewhat imposing on the child in devilish sport, she had been whetting the dagger that was to take her own life, and digging her own grave. It was then no wonder that she uttered a preternatural yell, and poured curses from the bottom of her heart. It must have been almost beyond human endurance, to hear the cry of her despair, and to witness the curses and the agony in which it vented itself.

Twenty-two years elapsed after this scene, when a wretched man, of the name of Edmund Robinson, conceived on the same spot the scheme of making himself a profitable speculation from a similar source. He trained his son, eleven years of age, and furnished him with the necessary instructions. He taught him to say that one day in the fields he had met with two dogs, which he urged on to hunt a hare. They would not budge; and he in revenge tied them to a bush and whipped them; when suddenly one of them was transformed into an old woman and the other into a child, a witch and her imp. This story succeeded so well, that the father soon after gave out that his son had an eye that could distinguish a witch by sight, and took him round to the neighbouring churches, where he placed him standing on a bench after service, and bade him look round and see what he could observe. The device, however clumsy, succeeded, and no less than seventeen persons were apprehended at the boy's selection, and conducted to Lancaster Castle. These seventeen persons were tried at the assizes, and found guilty; but the judge, whose name has unfortunately been lost, unlike Sir James Altham and Sir Edward Bromley, saw something in the case that excited his suspicion, and, though the juries had not hesitated in any one instance, respited the convicts, and sent up a report of the affair to the government. Twenty-two years on this occasion had not elapsed in vain. Four of the prisoners were by the judge's recommendation sent for to the metropolis, and were examined first by the king's physicians, and then by Charles the First in person. The boy's story was strictly scrutinised. In fine he confessed that it was all an imposture; and the whole seventeen received the royal pardon.

THE WITCH BAITER

Robert Anthony

Mynheer van Ragevoort did not like the dark. There were things he could not see in the dark, but which he knew were there. But there were also things that he knew did not exist, which the darkness nevertheless conjured before his eyes. Faces. Spectral figures that floated and threatened and mocked. Many faces, many figures. And those of women chiefly, and girls. Of course, they had been witches, and he had condemned them to the torture, to the stake, to the rope. But why should they trouble him, dance about him, beckon him? He had not executed them; he had merely been their judge, the administrator of the Law. The Law forced him, and he was helpless. Still they bothered. Sometimes they seemed so real . . .

Emphatically, Mynheer van Ragevoort, the Justice of Hegemonde, did not like the dark. Worse, noises often came from the night, noises that were mysterious and unaccountable. Sounds like the voices of people, especially sounds of women in pain, shrieking in torture, gasping brokenly.

There, the Justice started. He seemed to recognise a voice – yes, he heard it distinctly. It sounded like – ah, now he remembered – the voice of Melisande zer Honde, a slight girl, pale and pretty, a child of scarcely twelve. How she had screamed when the rack drew out her joints and stretched her muscles and ripped the ligaments. Yet she had confessed. He had been amazed that so young a child should be a witch. But witnesses had stated so, and under the torture she had admitted it. So he was forced to sentence her – to burning at the stake. How she had pleaded for life. How she had shrieked when the flames enveloped her. And then that appalling stillness, broken only by the crackling of faggots and the rush of flames.

And there was the sweet, innocent face of Gertrudis Bourdelaide. No, he doubted her accusers. He had known the girl since her birth; in fact he had lifted the child over the baptismal font as her godfather. Terrible she had been accused – and had confessed. They had to carry her away

24

from the torture. He remembered how her crushed legs had quivered in agony, the white bloodless features, the maimed hands. She had endured much, but she had confessed. The rope and quartering. But those moans, long-drawn, haunting, unending. Never a shriek, never a cry, only moans. Would he ever forget?

The Justice shook himself. He flung his cloak around his head and moved down the road, carrying in his hand a small lantern, from which a candle shone weakly. 'Not much good in this thick gloom,' he muttered. There was a fog in the air, which scarcely stirred with his movements. Yet the stillness, the lack of motion made him feel unsafe, restless. What was behind the gloom?

Hurriedly he trod the road toward his castle, his home. This stood somewhat apart from the city, as became the overlord and Justice. Not for him to live among gossips and small tradesmen. Besides, it was the home of his fathers.

A faint rustling sound made him pause. He peered around intently, but perceived nothing. Even his candle seemed unable to pierce the fog beyond his arm's reach. Silence around him. Well, he must move on, toward home, toward rest – perhaps. At least he would see his daughter . . .

Something huge and light fluttered from the fog and fell over his head, covering him with soft folds. In fright he dropped his lantern and gurgled a shriek. He fought back the folds, but they enveloped him tighter and tighter, drawing around him till his arms were helpless.

And then hands seized him, on the right and the left, and a voice whispered : 'Come ! But say naught.'

'What – what—' he began. But an insistent prod of some pointed weapon made him move forward.

Forward. But where? Where were they taking him? And for what purpose? The cloth covering his eyes made little difference; he had been unable to see anything without it. They left the road, moved across ditches, over the veldt. Stops when he was lifted over some obstacle – a hedge or boundary mark, he thought. More veldt. And around him the faint thuds of numerous feet, slithering noises of mantles brushing against each other, muffled clinks of metal. God. What was in store for him?

The Justice stumbled through a ditch. Then hard and rounded bumps under his feet – ah, he was back in Hegemonde, in the city among people. If he called—

s.w.—2

A sharp point pressed his side and a warning hiss apprised him of what would happen. So he was silent.

Some steps up which he stumbled, then a chamber. He felt himself led to a seat. How familiar that seat felt. With his feet he cautiously felt about himself. Yes, there were the legs of the table, and there his own footstool. It was his own : he was in the Court of Justice, his own court.

'Your own court. Your own dais,' came in deadened tones beside him. 'We are here to try the witch of witches, to try her under the Law. But she must not know us lest sorrow come to all of us. So speak not above a whisper.'

Routine. But why in the night? And who was the woman they called the witch of witches?

'Begin,' the dull command was given.

Routine. Well, he would go through with it. 'In the name of the Lord on High,' he intoned in a penetrating whisper, 'and in the name of His Majesty, the King of Spain and the Netherlands. There stands before us a – a—'

'A maiden,' prompted the voice.

' – a maiden, accused of having sold her immortal soul to the foul fiend in unholy conspiracy and of having exercised her black power in wanton sorcery and witchcraft to the detriment of man, woman and child, upon their property, their goods and possessions and upon their produce.' A pause, then : 'Woman, do you confess?'

Silence.

'Who witnesseth against her?' he continued.

'We all do witness against her,' whispered someone in front of him.

'Aye. Aye. It is true,' whispered many voices.

'We vow she hath bewitched us or those of our families and contributed to our loss, even the death of our loved ones,' said the accuser.

'Aye, she hath. We so vow it,' chorused the others.

'Doth the witch confess?' asked Mynheer the Justice.

Silence.

'Then to the rack with her – till she confesses.'

A scream of terror, quickly muffled, a sardonic cackle whose uvular tone seemed familiar, then the shuffle of many feet.

The Justice remained seated. No need for him to enter the torture chamber. Besides, he would not be able to see. In fact, he did not care to see. He had seen too many, too many. And they always confessed.

Through the open door he heard the spinning of rolls, the weak clatter of winding drums. A hush replete with indefinite sounds – they were fastening loops around the ankles and wrists of the witch. Then the squeak, a moan, a stifled shriek. A wait, then the splash of water. Another squeak of the drums . . .

In accustomed routine the Justice leaned to one side of the great chair. Another twist of the rack, then would come the familiar sounds, and then – confession. He listened inattentively. For there was a bigger, a personal question. What were they intending to do to him? And why this secret trial? If they would only talk in loud voices, and not in those awful whispers. It was unreal – unreal.

Again the splash of water, then another squeak, followed by faint clicks and tears, joints giving way and flesh ripping. A ghastly shriek. 'God. I confess,' in a pain-shocked voice. 'A-a-h-h,' and silence.

Yes, that was the usual result, sometimes a little slower in coming, but not often. There. That quiet crackle. He knew it. No wonder – the skilled hands of the executioner were in charge.

The shuffle of feet once more and then a voice :

'Your Worthiness, she hath confessed her guilt. Your sentence?'

Mynheer van Ragevoort roused himself. Sentence. Very well. 'To be hanged by the neck until death do claim her. At once.' This would be sufficient, and few preparations necessary. A rope and—

He must be short, he wanted to be away. Let them hurry and free him.

For a long time he sat there and waited – waited silently, for around him all noise had ceased. There had been a little shuffling of men entering the prison enclosure – to see the witch hung, of course – but nothing more. So he sat and pondered. He felt stifled. The cloth over his head impeded his breath, and drowsiness overcame him.

The tramp of feet aroused him. A moment later the fetters were removed from his arms and the cloth lifted from his head and shoulders.

He blinked in the sudden light of torches. Before him he saw a number of hooded figures, all with voluminous cloaks, faces hidden behind black veils. Were these the same men? he wondered.

'So it is here we find you, Sir Justice,' said the leader.

Mynheer did not recognise the voice.

'We looked for you in the castle. You were not there.'

Hm. So they looked for him. What did it mean? Why should they look for him when they had him already? And why no longer the whispers? At least he was thankful for that.

'Arise, sir, and take your place. You are to be tried,' said the leader.

Nine men in all, noted Mynheer. Two of them pushed him from the chair and led him down to a bench before the dais.

The tall leader at once occupied the chair of justice.

'Sir Justice, note what I say. You have been tried to execute sentence. We went to your home and waited for you. You did not come. Later we searched and found you absent. So at length we thought to look here. And here you are,' with sudden humour.

Mynheer van Ragevoort said nothing, only gazed bewildered at the speaker.

'Sir Justice, we are the Vehmgericht. In secret we met and considered you and the justice meted out by you. Sir, you have been an unjust judge. You have been a plague to this land. Like a wild beast you have persecuted the innocent and condemned them to death. Nothing has held you back – not friendship, not pity, not justice, not even the ties of blood. You lusted only to kill.'

He paused and seemed to wait for an objection.

Mynheer found the words. 'They were witches all. They confessed. The Law gave me—'

'The Law,' scorned the leader in stinging tones. 'Your wild superstition was the Law. Not the written Law. With you an accusation was the equal of proof. You never gave fair trial.'

'They confessed,' the Justice muttered.

The leader stood up and pointed an accusing finger at him. 'They confessed – under insane torture. They confessed – to escape further torture. They confessed – what you wished them to confess. Confession, indeed. So would you confess. Can an innocent child of ten – for such was Gertrudis Bourdelaide – know anything of wickedness, of sorcery, of witchcraft? Yet you forced her by the vilest tortures to say she was guilty. Did Melisande zer Honde know of witchcraft? She confessed to it – after you tore her on the rack. Did Roberta Deswaaters ever perpetrate any wickedness – she, a patient little saint, who spent most of her young life in pain? Yet you forced her to admit unholy practices – by means of the rack, the stocks. Did Margarete Van Voelker, or Pieta der Groote – oh, why name them all, the dozens of decent folk you put to death. For years you have sown terror in the land, you have revolted minds with your unheard-of cruelties. You were the scourge of the people until they wearied of it.

'Men came together and in secret protest asked the Vehmgericht for justice. When the Law is in unjust hands, man may, and must, take the Law from those hands and punish them. That is what the Vehmgericht has decided. Sir Justice, stand and hear your sentence.'

Mynheer van Ragevoort arose stiffly. It was all like a dream and still terribly real. For some reason he could not muster his thoughts to utter protest. Pictures of trials, of tortured women, of executions, raced through his mind. It was true, terribly true, what the leader had said. But he had not meant to be unjust. He, too, had suffered because of his duty. He had wanted to rid the land of the plague of witches, he had wished to make his land free of sorcery and witchery for all time to come. Many times he had wavered when friends, and even relatives, proved guilty; but resolutely, without fear or favour, he had administered the Law.

The leader was speaking. 'You were sentenced to torture and death,' he said in sombre tones. 'Such was the sentence decided on.'

A pause – Mynheer twisted his hands, his face suddenly pale and beaded with cold drops.

Again the leader spoke, solemnly, impressively, and the eyes that gleamed blackly through the veil held something of pity. 'Torture and death. Such was the sentence. But this sentence will not be carried out – not completely. You shall not die through our hands. For there is worse than death that has struck you. Perhaps it is the Hand of God. We assembled tonight to carry out the sentence on you. But we found that others had been at work. We found that they had seized you – grief-stricken fathers they were, men fully as crazed with fear of witches as you – they had captured the witch of witches, as they thought – had tried her before your court, tortured her and hung her. Their vengeance is gruesome.'

What did it all mean? Mynheer van Ragevoort seemed paralysed. His eyes were wide, his mouth open, all his features expressed complete lack of understanding.

'You know not,' continued the leader, 'who the witch of witches was? Nor will I tell you. They blinded you, Sir Justice, and blind was your judgment. But a taste of the torture shall be yours, and then you will be freed. Perhaps – perhaps you will be more forbearing hereafter. To work, men.'

Strong hands seized Mynheer van Ragevoort and quickly stripped him of his clothes. In a trice, so it seemed, they bore him to the torture chamber and looped the ropes around his wrists and ankles.

A spin of the drums, the ropes tautened and squeaked, pain unbearable shot through his limbs and scorched his joints.

'Another turn,' commanded the leader.

Agonised sweat rolled over the Justice's body, his mouth sagged and a croak came from his throat. 'I – I – confess,' he moaned.

'Confess,' exclaimed the leader in chill tones. 'Confess – what?'

The taut body could not even writhe – could only quiver. 'I – I – know not,' Mynheer gasped.

'Nor we.' The leader made a gesture, the drums swung back a half-turn and tightened with a jerk.

Suffering indescribable tore into him – the Justice fainted. Water, splashed over his head, awoke him. God. How he knew that crazing agony. He had sometimes wondered why the accused gave in so readily after a few whirls of the drums. He had been inclined to despise them as weaklings. Guilt alone could not endure, innocence certainly must. But now he knew. Oh, to escape this torment. Anything, anything – even death. But to escape.

A searing pain at his sides, yet he knew not whether it was hot or cold metal that touched him. And then the ropes became slack. What they did with him he scarcely knew – his whole body ached with tearing pains. And his head. It pounded and pounded and pounded.

A raw pain on his forefinger seemed to swell and swell until his arm – no, his body – grew large with the torment.

What were they doing? He saw it – a pincer was plucking at a fingernail – slowly pulling it from its foundation. God. What could he do to get away from such torture? Waves of pain welled forth from the finger, greater than his body could endure.

Something else. They had bound his wrists behind him; his ankles were also bound and heavy weights attached. Why this? Why didn't they simply kill him and be done with it.

A hook slipped under his fettered wrists, there was a pull, and suddenly he soared, his weighted body suspended by the wrists. And then he dropped. Again they drew him aloft and dropped him. Shoulders twisted and cracked and ached, his body seemed an immense pain. He fainted.

A rocking motion aroused him. He was dressed and covered with a cloth; they were carrying him. He felt strangely numb, conscious of ever-present but subdued pain. And so weary, so weak, so exhausted.

At last the motion changed. They had entered some dwelling, and now they laid him down. Steps moved away, and then someone spoke – the leader.

'The sentence had been executed, Sir Justice. May it teach you to be more merciful hereafter. We leave you now – with your victim.'

Half-conscious, he wondered. 'My victim?' he asked, his voice muffled by the enveloping cloth.

'Look and see,' in a chilling whisper. There were quick steps, the slam of a door, and then silence.

Mynheer van Ragevoort scrambled painfully to his feet, weakened hands tore at the enshrouding folds. There. He saw light – the cloth fell away. But he knew that room – those paintings – that table. So they had carried him to his house, his castle.

He was thankful for even that. But why this strange oppressive silence in the house? Where were the servants? And his—

His roving eye caught sight of something. Over there, on the great divan, lay something very limp and still, covered with a white drape. That – that – his victim, the leader had said. But in this house – was it – everything was so silent – was it his—? No, no, it must not be.

He crept weakly to the divan and tore the sheet from the still figure. 'God. Anne-Marie. My daughter.'

He stared at her, unbelieving, uncomprehending. His

victim? Oh, no. Not that, not that. But it was his daughter that lay there, lifeless, features frozen in an eternal mask.

Slowly he inspected her. Quivering fingers felt the soft flesh, not yet rigored in death. He saw raw welts around her wrists and bare ankles. Around her neck an irregular stripe – they had hanged her.

His victim. It was she – Anne-Marie, his daughter – that had been tried as the witch of witches that night. They had tortured her and – and he – he had ordered the torture. 'And she confessed,' he groaned, 'I – I – ordered her execution – as a witch! God!'

The room reeled and he crashed to the floor.

THE CHAMBRE ARDENTE AFFAIR

Ronald Seth

In the lay mind there is some confusion between what is meant by witchcraft and Black Magic, with which latter term is inextricably mixed the Blass Mass. It is, therefore, interesting to find that the first time the term Black Mass was used was in 1680, in a notorious case in France called the Chambre Ardente Affair.

The term holds terrible connotations. Even to the lukewarm Christian the idea that the Mass should be satirized with obscenities which scarcely bear contemplating, is too horrible to accept. Yet in the Chambre Ardente Affair the most obscene rites were performed, and the case which involved some of the most high-born in France, is one of the great high-lights in occult history.

Louis XIV had already been on the throne of France thirty-six years, and had another thirty-six years of his reign still to go, when rumours became rife of poisonings and on such a scale and involving such highly placed people at and around the Court that they could not be ignored. The King's mistress, Mme de Montespan, so it was whispered, was deeply mixed up in it, and as she was already slipping from the King's favour there was nothing to prevent her from being investigated at least. Though, in the event, she was not directly charged, the Affair gave Louis an opportunity for getting rid of several potential enemies, who might be termed her protégés.

The whole business actually had its roots in information laid to the police in 1673 by two fashionable confessors at Notre Dame de Paris. They did not mention any names, because of the secrecy of the confessional, but they assured the police that a large number of their penitents had confessed to them attempts to murder or actually-committed killings whose aim was to disentangle them from matrimonial triangles.

At the beginning the police were inclined to be sceptical of the two priests' tales. However, the Commissioner, Nicholas de la Reynie, ordered discreet inquiries to be made, as and when no more important business was in hand. To Reynie's surprise, and that of most of his senior colleagues, four years after the priests had first approached them, more or less by chance, the existence of a well-established poison ring was discovered. The ring had connections in England, Italy and Portugal, and was headed by a colourful figure, François Galaup de Chasteuil, son of the Attorney General of Aix, a Knight of Malta, and one-time Carmelite prior who had kept a mistress in his cell. Among its leading members were several nobles, a banker and a lawyer. Considerable stocks of poisons belonging to the gang were seized.

Chasteuil evaded capture, but the police arrested his accomplices. A year's questioning, however, failed to elicit information of any great significance. One of the suspects, a man called Vanens, later turned out to be the contact man for the petty distributors, the fortune-tellers who added to their meagre fees from this profession by acting as back-street abortionists and cheap prostitutes – and the sale of poisons.

It was not until the autumn of 1678 that the police had their first real break. Marie Bosse, a fortune-teller, was overheard by a detective confiding in a friend, 'I have such a good clientèle, so distinguished. No one lower than duchesses, princes, marquises and lords. When I have arranged three more poisonings I shall be able to retire and live on my fortune.'

When the detective reported to his superiors, it was decided not to dismiss the remarks as the boastings of a wishful-thinking old woman, and a woman detective was assigned to find out all she could about Mme Bosse and her shady business. She went to the fortune-teller and during the séance dropped a hint that she would like to do away with her husband.

'Nothing easier!' Mme Bosse assured her. 'If you can pay, that is.'

The agent could pay, and when she left she took with her a bottle of poison. The police pounced at once, and in Marie Bosse's apartment found a small stock of poisons.

Commissioner Reynie himself undertook the interrogation of Mme Bosse and began his questioning on 4th January, 1679. With Bosse had been arrested her two sons and her daughter, and another fortune-teller known as La Dame Vigoreux, who had been the mistress of the two former husbands of Marie Bosse. All five had lived together, to the extent of sharing the same bed.

What Reynie needed to put a stop to the sale of poisons was the names of customers of whom examples could be made, and who might lead to others. The first to fall to Reynie was a Madame de Poulaillon, a lady of quality if not titled.

Mme de Poulaillon had married a wealthy but aged husband, who proved not only impotent – that she did not mind – but a miser. At the instigation of a lover, she bought poison from La Bosse to get rid of her useless and mean spouse. The old man became suspicious, however, and took himself off to the safety of a monastery.

The method of poisoning taught by La Bosse – and others – was to soak the victim's shirt in a solution of arsenic, provided by her. This caused an inflammation of the skin resembling syphilis, to relieve which the wife bought an allegedly soothing ointment – also from La Bosse. Actually it was an ointment containing more poisons which, when rubbed into the skin, would bring about death in a few months.

Reynie's haul of suspects now began to snowball. During the following weeks several hundred of the leading courtiers were implicated and arrested. La Bosse had not, it seemed, been boasting.

Armed with this evidence the Commissioner was able to persuade Louis to give orders for the prosecution of the suspects. Because of the high rank of so many of them, and also because Mme de Montespan might quite possibly be involved, to reduce the scandal Louis decreed that a special Star Chamber court should be set up. All evidence was to be given *in camera*; there was to be no appeal against verdict or sentence.

This court subsequently became popularly known as La Chambre Ardente, because the room in which it sat was draped in black and lit with candles.

Somewhat unprofessionally, perhaps, La Bosse implicated a fellow fortune-teller, the celebrated chiromancer and physiognomist, whose services were much sought by the *beau monde*, Catherine Deshayes (alias the Widow Montvoisin) commonly known as La Voisin. La Voisin retorted with further allegations against La Bosse.

Caught up in the accusations and counter-accusations of

these two jealous old women were the widows of two Paris magistrates. They were arrested on charges of having bought poison from La Voisin.

Another accomplice of La Voisin, the abortionist La Lepère, was also imprisoned. In vain did she plead that she only helped those whose menstruation was delayed, not those who were pregnant, nor would she take money from virgins who believed they were pregnant. Several witnesses alleged that the two women had buried large numbers of foetuses and unwanted babies in a garden in the Paris suburb of Villeneuve-sur-Gravois, one actually charging La Voisin of having disposed of more than 2,500 little corpses in this way.

Hoping to dispose of the case quickly, the Chambre Ardente sentenced La Bosse and La Vigoreux to death at the stake, and Bosse's son François to hanging. Mme de Poulaillon was banished, and judgment on Vanens, the distributor of the poisons, La Voisin and La Lepère was deferred.

Up to this point, witchcraft had not been involved, though sorcery had certainly been, for the fortune-tellers and abortionists had sold love philtres and mixed their arsenic, sulphur and vitriol with the dried blood of bats and toads, semen and menstrual discharge. Later evidence also did not introduce witchcraft, for it concerned chiefly the suspected roles of the ladies-in-waiting to the King's various favourites as poison distributors. One of those caught up in the affair in the autumn of 1679 was Jean Racine, the playwright, against whom a warrant was issued, though it was never served, on the grounds that he had murdered his mistress.

As time passed more and more members of the Court became involved. On 23rd January, 1680, the Chambre ordered the arrest of the Comtesse de Soissons, the Marquise d'Alluye, Mme de Polignac, one of the King's mistresses, Mme de Tingry, the Duchess of Bouillon, the Marquise du Roure, the Duke of Luxembourg (Captain of the King's Guard) and the Marquis de Feuquières. As may be imagined, all high society was in an uproar. A number of the accused fled France.

The Duchess of Bouillon was accompanied to court by her lover and by the husband whom she was accused of trying to murder. She testified that she did not know La Vigoreux, but was acquainted with La Voisin, whom she consulted from time to time, because 'you have to tread warily these days.' As she left the court, she was heard to remark, 'Truly, I would never have believed such intelligent men could ask such stupid questions.'

Many were now rapidly coming to the opinion of the Marquis de Pas, who had declared that a number of professional poisoners of both sexes who had come under the rigour of the law had hit upon an easy way of prolonging their lives by denouncing various aristocrats at intervals, the interrogation of whom 'gives these wretches a little more time.'

Commissioner Reynie, realising the degree of antagonism that was building up against him, decided to press his low-class prisoners. In particular he concentrated on a former convict from the galleys, a man called Lesage, who turned King's Evidence.

Despite three days of intense pain caused by the *sellette* – the torture chair – and the *brodequins* – wedges hammered into boots which crushed the legs – La Voisin denied all charges of poisoning. The court transcript records her shrieks at each successive crushing of her legs, and remarks, 'Mais elle ne dit rien' – 'But she says nothing.'

Reynie believed that she refused to talk because the tortures were not severe enough. The Attorney General demanded the cutting out of her tongue and the chopping off of her hands, but the court was content to condemn her to the stake.

By this time witchcraft had been introduced. Lesage had accused two priests, Father Davot and Father Mariette, of saying Black Masses on the bellies of naked girls. The priest of St. Sauveur, Father Gérard, was accused of saying a similar mass, with the added detail that he copulated with the girl who was serving as his altar, during it.

It is significant, however, that it was only after Reynie began to use torture that the accusations of witchcraft began to amount to anything. The tortures he most frequently used were the rack and the *question de l'eau*, in which eight pitchers of water were poured down the victim's throat. At one time he considered calling Madeleine Bavent, one of the leading figures in the case of the Louviers Nuns, but the court forbade it.

On 24th February, 1680, the Chambre Ardente had its terms of reference extended to include sacrilege, impiety and profanation.

Father Mariette was arrested at Toulouse and brought to Paris, to face the accusation of Lesage and La Voisin's daughter that he had sacrificed white pigeons and had made wax figures. La Filastre, another fortune-teller, admitted that she had sacrificed a child to the Devil standing in a circle of black candles, while renouncing the sacraments. At one Black Mass celebrated by Father Deshayes and Father Cotton, she had sacrificed her own newborn baby, and one of the priests had said a mass over the placenta.

Father Davot had said an amatory mass over a naked girl, throughout which he had continually kissed the girl's genitals. In the woods at Fontainebleau, Mme de Lusignan and her confessor, naked, had practised abominable rites with a large Easter candle. Father Tournet said three amatory masses, during one of which he had publicly copulated with the girl on the altar.

Father Guibourg, the sixty-six year old son of Henri de Montmorency, was charged with being an accomplice of La Voisin at whose request he had said a placenta mass for Mlle la Coudraye. At other masses celebrated on the bodies of naked women, at the elevation of the Host he had inserted conjurations for hidden treasure or for sexual attraction.

La Voisin's daughter corroborated his own evidence that at another mass he had murdered a child of his three mistresses, Jeanne Chaufrain, by whom he had seven children.

Guibourg had also celebrated an amatory mass for one of the King's mistresses, Mlle des Oeillets. The account goes : 'In fur stole and manciple he had read a conjuration in the presence of Mlle des Oeillets, who was preparing a charm to secure to herself the King's love. She was accompanied by a gentleman who gave him the words of the conjuration. For this rite it was necessary to have the seed of both sexes, but as Mlle des Oeillets was having her monthly period, she put some menstrual blood into the chalice instead. The gentleman who was with her went into the space between the bed and the wall and stimulated himself, and Guibourg directed his semen into the chalice. Into this mixture, each placed a powder from the blood of bats, and added some flour to give it a firm consistency. Then Guibourg recited the conjuration, and poured what was in the chalice into a little bottle, which Mlle des Oeillets and the gentleman took away with them.'

All these obscene rites were merely an extension of two

centuries' belief in witchcraft, which had evolved out of earlier theories of the great powers of the Devil. From this conception, in which the good God counteracted the bad Devil, there developed a kind of dualism, in which obscene rites became entangled with orthodox ritual.

La Voisin, for example, was arrested as she was coming from Mass on a Sunday morning. La Lepère never failed to baptise the still-born babies she procured for the Black Masses. The high-born and intelligent involved in the case were behaving on the level of peasants when they sought help from friends of the Devil. Masses of special intention have always been said – for the repose of a soul, for success in specified undertakings, for health – and to extend such intentions to love was not, therefore, considered illogical.

In fact, though Reynie was convinced of the rightness of the cases he made out against his suspects, in any other court all the evidence given by them would have been considered worthless, chiefly because they were men and women of low reputation. Not until torture was introduced into the proceedings were any sensational revelations made. Even under torture La Voisin steadfastly denied all charges of witchcraft, and La Filastre retracted her confession made under torture before she went to the stake, declaring that 'everything she had said in this respect had been only to free herself from the pain and agony of the torture and in fear lest it be continued' – a prominent feature of many witchcraft trials that took place between 1450 and 1750 all over Europe.

On the other hand, very convincing evidence of witchcraft practices was found in the fortune-tellers' houses. There were wax figures, charms of all kinds, books on magic and black candles – all the paraphernalia of witchcraft. Perhaps the most damning evidence against Father Guibourg were the receipts for large sums of money paid to him for his services.

By 1680 the Black Mass, complete with nude bellies and babies' blood in the chalice, and a black host, and black candles was the latest thing.

There is no doubt that the Chambre Ardent Affair was the greatest French scandal of the century, and Louis was faced with the problem of trying to cover it up as much as possible. In August 1680 he suspended the Chambre, chiefly because the scandal was coming too close to home. Reynie had uncovered evidence tending to show that Mme de Montespan had attempted to poison his new young mistress, Mlle de Fontagnes.

The King, nevertheless, instructed Reynie to continue his investigations, but in the greatest secrecy, and as time went by it became all too apparent that Mme de Montespan was the fountain-head of all this witchcraft and Black Magic, which increased even further the need for secrecy. For two more years Reynie continued to arrest, torture and burn many men and women of the lower classes accused of supplying poison and practising witchcraft. But no aristocratic victim was tortured or executed.

During the four years 1678 to 1682, 319 people were arrested; 104 were sentenced – thirty-six to death, four to the galleys, thirty-four to banishment, and thirty were acquitted. Legislation was introduced banning fortune-tellers and declaring witchcraft to be a superstition. In 1709 Louis decided to destroy the records, and on 13th July they were burned. But somehow copies of the official transcripts and Reynie's notes escaped destruction. These notes and transcripts are now in the archives of the Bibliothèque Nationale.

THE INITIATION TO WITCHCRAFT

Margaret Murray

In all organised religions there is some form of admission into the cult by which a candidate can become a member. Often there are two forms, the first when a young infant is received, the other when at puberty the candidate takes on himself the full membership. For an adult convert the two ceremonies are combined with the necessary modifications. In these respects the Witch-religion, i.e. the cult of the Horned God, conforms to the ordinary routine of all religions.

The form for the admission of infants is best recorded in France. The mother took her young child to one of the great quarterly Sabbaths, and kneeling before the Incarnate God she said, 'Great Lord, whom I worship, I bring thee a new servant who will be thy slave for ever.' At a sign from the god she moved forward on her knees and laid the infant in the divine arms. Such a ceremony, at once simple and touching, must have had a great effect on the minds of the mothers; they saw with their own eyes that the god himself had received the child. In some places the infant was also baptised with water, and at Orleans chrism was used.

All the inquisitors and other recorders mention that the 'witches' were exceedingly careful to have their children received by their god, and to bring them up in the tenets and practice of the Pagan religion. Such an attitude of mind would have brought nothing but praise had the parents been of the same religion as the recorders and judges, but as the parents belonged to another faith their action in the matter was regarded as essentially wicked. The French inquisitors were peculiarly horrified at the numbers of children dedicated to non-Christian deity, 'witches were accustomed to have their children baptised more often at the Sabbath than in church, and presented more often to the Devil than to God.' In 1578 Jeanne Hervillier, who was from Verberie, near Compiègne, deposed that from her birth she was dedicated to the Devil by her mother. Boguet in 1598 relates that Pierre Willermoz, being only ten years old, was taken by his father to the Sabbath, and that three other very young children were taken in the same way by their maternal grandmother. In the Home for poor girls founded by Madame Bourignon at Lille, one of the girls told Madame Bourignon in 1661 that 'her mother had taken her with her when she was very young and had even carried her in her arms to the Witches' Sabbath'. Another girl, still younger, had been a constant attendant at the Sabbath since she was a little child. Madame Bourignon, who was a deeply religious Christian, was shocked at the ignorance of Christianity displayed by the girls under her care, and records that they were 'for the most part so ignorant of the fact of their salvation that they lived like animals'.

If in the course of a trial it transpired that an accused had been thus dedicated in infancy it was proof positive that he or she came of a witch family, which was in itself such strong presumptive evidence of witch propensities that few, if any, escaped after the fact came to light. Reginald Scot is very definite on this point; quoting from Bodin he says, 'Witches must be examined, whether their parents were witches or no, for witches come by propagation.' In another place he quotes from Cornelius Agrippa that 'in Brabant a woman was accused as a witch and one of the proofs against her was that her mother was in times past burned for a witch.' Jeanne Hervillier's mother was burnt as a witch long before Jeanne herself was accused. One of the strong proofs of witchcraft against Elizabeth Clarke in Essex in 1645 was that her mother and some other of her kinsfolk 'did suffer death for witchcraft and murder'. The mother and aunt of Alexander Sussums of Melford, in Suffolk, in 1645 were both hanged and his grandmother burnt for being witches; 'so were others of them questioned and hanged.' Everywhere the 'witchbrood' received scant mercy at the hands of the authorities.

When the child was old enough to understand, an age which varied from nine to thirteen years, he made a public profession of faith. This was not necessarily at a great Sabbath, but had to be done before witnesses. The candidate prostrated himself on the ground at the feet of the Divine Man who asked, 'Dost thou come of thy own free will?' The candidate replied, 'Yes.' The god then said, 'Do what I desire and what I do.' The candidate still kneeling made the profession of faith, 'Thou art my god and I am thy slave.' Homage was then rendered to the god, and the novice was marked on some part of the person so that he might be known by others as a full member. The mark was either a scar or a tattoo. These ceremonies are paralleled in modern times among many races, the physical mark being often an essential part of the proceedings. Madame Bourignon says, 'When a child offered to the Devil by its Parents, comes to the use of Reason, the Devil then demands its soul and makes it deny God and renounce its Baptism, and all relating to the Faith, promising Homage and Fealty to the Devil in manner of a Marriage, and instead of a Ring, the Devil gives them a Mark with an iron Awl in some part of the Body.' Bodin notes that 'fathers and mothers consecrate and dedicate their children to the Devils, some when they are newly born, others while still unborn. The Devils do not make express paction with the children vowed to them until they reach the age of puberty.' Elizabeth Francis, tried at Chelmsford in 1556, was taught 'the art of witchcraft', i.e. her religion, by her grandmother when she reached the age of twelve. Elizabeth Demdike, the most celebrated of all the Lancashire witches, 'brought up her own children, instructed her grandchildren, and took great care and pains to bring them to be Witches.' Had Elizabeth Demdike been a Christian she would have been held up to admiration as a pattern of what a pious and devout woman should be. At Paisley, Annabil Stuart was fourteen when at her mother's insistence she made the vows to the Devil. In this connection it may be noted that Joan of Arc was twelve years old when she first began to take an active part in her religion, and that much of her religious instruction came from the godmother who had dealings with the fairies.

The rites for the admission of an adult convert were more dramatic than those for a boy or girl already belonging to the religion. The accounts are fuller as the records were made when the cult of the Horned God was already waning and had to keep up its numbers by proselytising. As in all admissions to a new religion the convert had to renounce his old faith, and this renunciation was made as explicit as possible. 'I renounce and deny God, the blessed Virgin, the Saints, baptism, father, mother, relations, heaven, earth, and all that is in the world', was one of several formulae; which always had to be 'an express renunciation of Jesus Christ and of the Faith'. Then came the baptism, the profession of faith and the vow of fidelity, 'I place myself at every point in thy power and in thy hands, recognizing no other god, for thou art my god.' A variant of the vow of fidelity much used in Scotland was that the candidate placed one hand on the crown of her head, the other under the sole of her foot, and dedicated all that was between the two hands to the service of her god. The solemn vow of self-dedication to the deity actually present in person must have been peculiarly impressive. The Swedish witches had a special rite which was obviously intended to impress ignorant minds. They were given a little bag containing a few shavings of a clock to which a stone was tied; they threw this into the water, saying, 'As these shavings of the clock do never return to the clock from which they are taken, so may my soul never return to heaven.' This renunciation of a previous religion is noted as early as 1584 by Reginald Scot, who was one of the first to raise his voice against the persecution by Christians of the heathen in their midst, 'As our witches are said to renounce Christ and despite his sacraments : so do the other forsake Mahomet and his lawes.'

After the renunciation of his old religion the convert advanced to the actual admission ceremony, which consisted of baptism and marking. Baptism was the less important part in the eyes of the members of the cult and was often omitted. It was, however, a rite which was in force before the introduction of Christianity and has therefore a definite bearing on the antiquity of the religion of the Horned God. Adult baptism, as recorded in the New Testament, was apparently performed by immersion in a river, but the witch-baptism varied from dipping the head in water to a mere sprinkling; total immersion is never recorded. The rite must have been general through Western and Central Europe, as Sir George Mackenzie quotes Delrio to the effect that 'the Devil useth to Baptise them of new, and to wipe off their Brow their old Baptism'. In France baptism of children only is noted, and it is a remarkable fact that baptism either of adults or children is never mentioned in English trials though it is recorded in New England. Adult baptism is found in the accounts from Scotland and Sweden. The earliest is from Bute in 1669, when several witches gave evidence; Margret McLevine said, 'He asked, what was her name. She answered him, Margret, the name that God gave me, and he said to her, I baptise thee Jonet'; Isobel McNicoll confessed that 'he bap-

44

tised her and gave her a new name and called her Caterine';
Jonet McNicoll, 'confesses with remorse' that she met 'a
gross copper-faced man, whom she knew to be an evil spirit,
and that he gave her a new name, saying, I baptise thee
Mary'; Jonet Morisoun 'trysted with the Devil, and he asked
what was her name, and she answered, Jonet Morisoun, the
name that God gave me, and he said, believe not in Christ
but believe in me. I baptise thee Margaret.' In Sweden the
converts had to make an oath of fidelity on the occasion of
the baptism, 'he caused them to be baptised by such Priests
as he had there, and made them confirm their Baptism with
dreadful Oaths and Imprecations'. The 'oaths and imprecations' are recorded by Boguet in a more reasonable manner,
'He makes them give up their part in Paradise [i.e. the
Christian heaven], and makes them promise that they will
hold him as their sole master for ever, and that they will
always be faithful to him. Above all, he makes them swear
very solemnly that they will never accuse one another, nor
report anything which has passed among them.' In New
England baptism is recorded as being practised regularly.
Mary Osgood said that 'she was baptised by the Devil, who
dipped her face in the water, and made her renounce her
former baptism, and told her she must be his, soul and body,
for ever and ever'. Goody Lacey saw six baptised, 'he dipped
their heads in the water, saying, they were his.'

The kiss often followed the baptism. The new member
kissed the Grandmaster on any part of his person that he
directed. This was in token of absolute subjection, such as
was found in the Middle Ages in the kissing of the Pope's
foot or the kissing of the hand of a monarch. The recorders,
however, disregarded the Christian parallels, and make a
great feature of the kiss as being most humiliating.

The marking of the new convert was another ceremony
which appealed to the imagination of the recorders, and is
therefore described in some detail. *The Mysterie of Witchcraft*, written in 1617, tells us that 'the Devil sets his seale
upon them. This is commonly some sure marke in some secret
place of their bodies, which shall remain sore and unhealed
until his next meeting with them, and then for afterwards
prove ever insensible.' The author of *The Lawes against
Witches and Conjuration*, published 'By Authority' in 1645,
states that 'the Devil leaveth marks upon their bodies, sometimes like a Blew-spot, or a Red-spot like a flea-biting'. Sir

George Mackenzie, the great Scotch lawyer, writing on the legal aspect of the subject, says, 'The Devil's Mark useth to be a great Article with us, but it is not *per se* found relevant, except it be confest by them, that they got that Mark with their own consent; *quo casu*, it is equivalent to a paction. The Mark is given to them, as is alledg'd, by a Nip in any part of the body, and it is blew.'

The evidence shows that the mark was caused by pricking or cutting the skin till blood came; the operator then passed his hand over the wound, there was a considerable amount of pain which lasted some days or even longer; when the wound healed the resultant red or blue mark was indelible. This process is obviously some form of tattooing, and is perhaps the attenuated survival of the ancient British and Pictish custom of tattooing the whole body with blue pigment, a custom which among the witches was not confined to Great Britain, but extended to the Continent as well, particularly to France.

There was no special place on the body on which the mark was made, though Boguet says that it was usually on the left shoulder. De Lancre says that in his part of the country the left side and the left shoulder were marked, that the skin was torn to the effusion of blood, and that the pain might last for three months. He also says that there was a sensation of heat which penetrated into the flesh. Jeanne d'Abadie told de Lancre that when the Devil marked her on the right shoulder he hurt her so much that she cried out, and felt at the time a great heat as if a fire had burned her. The marking of witches in other countries was not so dramatically recorded. The Belgian witch, Elisabeth Vlamynx, tried in 1595, merely stated that she was marked on the left armpit. Two witches tried at Aberdeen in 1597 confessed to the Devil's marks, Andro Man that 'Christsonday bit a mark in the third finger of thy right hand, which thou hast yet to show', and Christian Mitchell that 'the Devil gave thee a nip on the back of thy right hand, for a mark that thou was one of his number'. Sylvine de la Plaine, a young married woman aged twenty-three, confessed at Brécy in 1616 that she had been marked on the crown of the head and on the right thigh. The Yarmouth witch, tried in 1644, saw a tall black man at her door, 'he told her he must see her Hand; and then taking out something like a Pen-knife, he gave it *a little Scratch* so that Blood followed, and the *Mark* remained to that time'. The Essex witch, Rebecca Jones, told the magistrates that a handsome young man came to the door whom 'now she thinks was the devil; who asked this examinate how she did and desired to see her left wrist, which she showed unto him; and he then took a pin from his examinant's own sleeve, and pricked her wrist twice, and there came a drop of blood, which he took off with the top of his finger, and so departed'. The Forfar witches, tried in 1661, were marked on the shoulder, Jonet Howat said that 'the devil nipped her upon her shoulders, so as she had great pain for some time thereafter', that when he came again he 'stroked her shoulder (which he had nipped) with his hand, and that presently after she was eased of her former pain'. Another witch of the same coven was also nipped in the same way; four weeks later 'the devil stroked her shoulder with his fingers, and after that she had ease in the place formerly nipped by the Devil'. Marie Lamont of Innerkip, in 1662, stated that 'the Devil nipped her on the right side which was very painful for a time, but thereafter he stroked it with his hand, and healed it; this she confesses to be his mark'. In Bute in 1662, Margaret McWilliam, who seems to have been one of the chief witches there, was marked in three places, one near her left shin-bone, another between her shoulders, and the third on the hip, all of them blue marks. Margret McLevine, of the same coven, stated that the Devil came to her, 'he took her by the middle finger of the right hand which he had almost cut off her, and therewith left her. Her finger was so sorely pained for the space of a month thereafter that there was no pain comparable to it, as also took her by the right leg which was sorely pained likewise as also by the Devil.' Three of the Wincanton witches were found to be marked at their trial in 1664; 'he prickt the fourth Finger of Elizabeth Style's right hand between the middle and upper joynt (where the sign at the Examination remained)'; in the case of Alice Duke, 'he prickt the fourth finger of her right hand between the middle and upper joynt (where the mark is yet to be seen)'; and in the case of Christian Green, 'the Man in Black prickt the fourth finger of thy Right hand between the middle and upper joints, where the sign yet remains'. Annabil Stuart of Paisley, who was only fourteen when tried in 1678, said that 'the Devil took her by the Hand and nipped her Arm, which continued to be sore for half an hour'. At Borrowstrowness, in 1679, Margaret Pringle stated that the Devil

47

took her by the right hand 'whereby it was grievously pained; but having it touched of new again, it immediately became whole'. Little Thomas Lindsay, of Renfrewshire, when he joined the coven, had 'a Nip on the Neck, which continued sore for Ten days'; and John Reid, who later suffered the traitor's death in prison, received 'a Bite or Nipp in his Loyn, which he found painfull for a Fortnight'. Isobel Adams of Pittenweem, said at her trial in 1704, that 'the Devil put his mark in her flesh which was very painful'. In 1705 the two Northampton witches, Elinor Shaw and Mary Phillips, who like the rest of that coven remained faithful to their god unto death, had been pricked at their finger ends.

The Pact or Covenant was probably a late custom, introduced when the religion was falling into decay. In all religions the god promises to the convert eternal life and eternal happiness in return for fidelity and service, but the promise of mundane help enforced by a written contract suggests a form of propaganda which could only have occurred when the religion was hard pressed for converts. The written contract was the most important part of the admission ceremony in the eyes of the legal authorities who tried the witches; it appeared to give an air of finality to the whole transaction. Occasionally, especially in France, one of these written covenants fell into the hands of the inquisitors; unfortunately the exact wording is never given in the records, the inquisitor preferring to make his readers' flesh creep by saying that 'it was so horrible that one had horror in seeing it.' In England and Scotland there is no record of such a contract having been brought into court as evidence against an accused person; it would appear that the Devil kept the paper in some secure place and perhaps destroyed it if there were danger.

No contract was signed without the free consent of the contracting parties, as is clearly shown in many of the trials; the Devil always asked the candidate whether he or she wished to become his servant and the paper was not produced unless the answer was very definitely in the affirmative. If the witch could not write she signed the paper with a cross or circle, or the Devil put his hand on hers and guided her hand in signing her name. The signing is usually said to have been done with the blood of the witch drawn from some part of her person for the purpose; this is, however, merely a confusion with the marking of the candidate when the skin was cut to the effusion of blood. In the later rite, the blood was a convenient fluid for writing the signature when ink was a rare commodity, as is always the case in country places. It is possible also that the blood thus drawn may have been regarded as an offering to the new god. The contract was originally made out and signed on a separate piece of parchment or paper; in the later trials it was said to be in a book, but this is probably a confusion with the Devil's book in which the records were made at the Sabbaths. In America the book was constantly mentioned by the parsons and ministers who recorded the trials. Forbes, in his *Institutes of the Law of Scotland*, says 'An express Covenant is entered into betwixt a Witch and the Devil appearing in some visible Shape. Whereby the former renounceth God and His Baptism, engages to serve the Devil, and do all the Mischief he can as Occasion offers, and leaves his Soul and Body to his Disposal after Death. The Devil on his Part articles with such Proselytes concerning the Shape he is to appear to them in, the Services they are to expect from him, upon the Performance of certain Charms or ceremonious Rites'. Claire Goessen, a Belgian witch tried in 1603, made a covenant with the Devil, 'this pact was written on paper by Satan himself with blood taken from a prick which she made for that purpose with a pin in the thumb of her left hand, and was signed by the prisoner with her own blood'. Half a century later, in 1657, a Belgian man-witch named Mathieu Stoop, signed a pact with blood drawn from his right leg, but was marked at the same time in the right armpit.

Various methods of making a pact with the Devil were in vogue in France, Belgium and Wales until a recent period. In Belgium the would-be candidate goes to a cross-road at night carrying a black hen. The Devil in the form of a man will come and bargain for the hen, then will buy it by giving the seller what he desires. The pact is made for the duration of seven years. In the Department of Entre-Sambre-et-Meuse, the ritual is slightly different: 'Come to the wood and you will see a man coming to you. This is the chief. He will ask if you will engage in his society. If you refuse he will tell you to return whence you came. If you accept, the term of the engagement is for seven years, and you will get a *plaquette* a day.' The Welsh method carries on the idea of the magical power of the Host. In North Pembrokeshire an old man-witch gave an account of how he obtained his power. When he went to his first Communion he made pretence of eating the bread 'and then put it in his pocket. When he went forth from the service there was a dog meeting him by the gate, to which he gave the bread, thus selling his soul to the Devil. Ever after, he possessed the power to bewitch.'

The contract between the Devil and the witch was generally for the term of the witch's life, but contracts for a term of years are often found. Records and tradition agree in stating that the number of years was seven, though there is some evidence that nine years was also a favourite number. At the end of the term the witch was at liberty to refuse to renew it. The length of the term suggests that it was connected with the cycle of years for the Great Sacrifice in which the god himself was the Divine Victim. If this theory is correct it means that the witch was the substitute for the god, and explains why in so many cases the Devil promised that she should have power and riches during the interval before the end came. In all records of the substitute for the Divine Victim the mock king is allowed the royal power for a certain length of time before the sacrifice is consummated. This I take to be the meaning of the numerous stories of persons selling their souls for the sake of being rich for a term of years and being killed by the Devil at the end of that term.

THE SPELL OF WITCHCRAFT

P. T. Barnum

Witchcraft is one of the most baseless, absurd, disgusting and silly of all the humbugs. And it is not a dead humbug either; it is alive, busily exercised by knaves and believed by fools all over the world. Witches and wizards operate and prosper among the Hottentots and negroes and barbarous Indians, among the Siberians and Kirgishes and Lapps, of course. Everybody knows *that* – they are poor ignorant creatures! Yes: but are the French, and Germans, and English, and Americans poor ignorant creatures too? They are, if the belief and practice of witchcraft among them is any test; for in all those countries there are witches. I take up one of the New York City dailies of this very morning, and find in it the advertisements of seven witches. In 1858, there were in full blast in New York and Brooklyn sixteen witches and two wizards. One of these wizards was a black man; a very proper style of person to deal with the black art.

Witch, means a woman who practises sorcery under an agreement with the devil, who helps her. Before the Christian era, the Jewish witch was a mere diviner, or at most a raiser of the dead, and the Gentile witch was a poisoner, a maker of philtres or love potions, and a vulgar sort of magician. The devil part of the business did not begin until a good while after Christ. During the last century or so, again, while witchcraft has been extensively believed in, the witch has degenerated into a very vulgar and poverty-stricken sort of conjuring woman. Take our New York City witches, for instance. They live in cheap and dirty streets that smell bad; their houses are in the same style, infected with a strong odour of cabbage, onions, washing-day, old dinners, and other merely sublunary smells. Their rooms are very ill furnished, and often beset with wash-tubs, swill-pails, mops, and soiled clothes; their personal appearance is commonly unclean, homely, vulgar, coarse and ignorant, and often rummy. Their fee is a quarter or half of a dollar. Sometimes a dollar. Their divination is worked by cutting and dealing cards or studying the palm of your hand. And the things which they tell you are the most silly and shallow babble in the world; a mess of phrases worn out over and over again. Here is a specimen, as gabbled to the customer over a pack of cards laid out on the table; anybody can do the like : 'You face a misfortune. I think it will come upon you within three weeks, but it may not. A dark-complexioned man faces your life-card. He is plotting against you, and you must beware of him. Your marriage-card faces two young women, one fair and the other dark. One you will have, and the other you will not. I think you will have the fair one. She favours the dark-complexioned man, which means trouble. You face money, but you must earn it. There is a good deal, but you may not get much of it,' &c., &c. These words are exactly the sort of stuff that is sold by the witches of today.

Other countries are favoured in like manner. I have not just now the most recent information, but in the year 1857 and 1858, for instance, mobbing and prosecutions growing out of a popular belief in witchcraft were quite plentiful enough in various parts of Europe. No less than eight cases of the kind in England alone were reported during those two years. Among them was the actual murder of a woman as a witch by a mob in Shropshire; and an attack by another mob in Essex, upon a perfectly inoffensive person, on suspicion of having 'bewitched' a scolding, ill-conditioned girl, from which attack the mob was diverted with much difficulty, and thinking itself very unjustly treated. Some others of those cases show a singular quantity of credulity among people of respectability.

While, therefore, some of us may perhaps be justly thankful for safety from such horrible follies as these, still we cannot properly feel very proud of the progress of humanity, since, after not less than six thousand years of existence, and eighteen hundred of revelation, so many believers in witchcraft still exist among the most civilized nations.

It is worth while to print in plain English for my readers a good selection of the very words which have been believed, or are still believed, to possess magic power. Then, any who choose, may operate by themselves, or may put some bold friend up in a corner, and blaze away at him or her until they are wholly satisfied about the power of magic.

The Roman Cato, so famous for his grimness and virtue, believed that if he were ill, it would much help him, and that it would cure sprains in others, to say over these words : 'Daries, dardaries, astaris, ista, pista, sista'; or, as another account has it, 'motas, daries, dardaries, astaries'; or, as still another account says, 'Huat, huat, huat; ista, pista, sista; domiabo, damnaustra.' And sure enough, nothing is truer, as any physician will tell you, that if the old censor only believed hard enough, it would almost certainly help him; not by the force of the words, but by the force of his own ancient Roman imagination. Here are some Greek words of no less virtue : '*Aski, Kataski, Tetrax.*' When the Greek priests let out of their doors those who had been completely initiated in the Eleusinian mysteries, they said to them last of all the awful and powerful words, '*Konx, ompax.*' If you want to know what the usual result was, just say them to somebody, and you will see instantly. The ancient Hebrews believed that there was a secret name of God, usually thought to be inexpressible, and only to be represented by a mystic figure kept in the Temple, and that if anyone could learn it, and repeat it, he could rule the intelligent and unintelligent creation at his will. It is supposed by some that Jehovah is the word which stands for this secret name; and some Hebraists think that the word 'Yahveh' is much more nearly the right one. The Mohammedans, who have received many notions from the Jews, believe the same story about the secret name of God, and they think it was engraved on Solomon's signet, as all readers of the *Arabian Nights* will very well remember. The Jews believed that if you pronounced the word 'Satan', any evil spirit that happened to be by could in consequence instantly pop into you if he wished, and possess you, as the devils in the New Testament possessed people.

Some ancient cities had a secret name, and it was believed that if their enemies could find this out, they could conjure with it so as to destroy such cities. Thus, the secret name of Rome was Valentia, and the word was very carefully kept, with the intention that none should know it except one or two of the chief pontiffs.

Mr. Borrow, in one of his books, tells about a charm which a gipsy woman knew and which she used to repeat to herself as a means of obtaining supernatural aid when she happened to want it. This was, 'Saboca enrecar Maria ereria.' He induced her, after much effort, to repeat the words to him, but she always wished she had not, with an evident conviction that some harm would result. He explained to her that they consisted of a very simple phrase, but it made no difference.

An ancient physician, named Serenus Sammonicus, used to be quite sure of curing fevers by means of what he called Abracadabra, which was a sort of inscription to be written on something and worn on the patient's person. It was as follows :

ABRACADABRA
BRACADABR
RACADAB
ACADA
CAD
A

Another gentleman of the same school used to cure sore eyes by hanging round the patient's neck an inscription made up of only two letters, A and Z; but how he mixed them we unfortunately do not know.

By the way, many of the German peasantry in the more ignorant districts still believe that to write Abracadabra on a slip of paper and keep it with you, will protect you from wounds, and that if your house is on fire, to throw this strip into it will put the fire out.

Many charms or incantations call on God, Christ, or some saints, just as the heathen ones call on a spirit. Here is one for epilepsy that seems to appeal to both religions, as if with a queer proviso against any possible mistake about either. Taking the epileptic by the hand, you whisper in his ear, 'I adjure thee by the sun and the moon and the gospel of today, that thou arise and no more fall to the ground; in the name of the Father, son, and Holy Ghost.'

A charm for the cramp, found in vogue in some rustic regions, is this :

> 'The devil is tying a knot in my leg,
> Mark, Luke, and John, unloose it, I beg
> Crosses three we make to ease us –
> Two for the thieves, and one for Christ Jesus.'

Here is another, often used in Ireland, which in the same spirit of superstition and ignorant irreverence uses the name of the Saviour for a slight human occasion. It is to cure the toothache, and requires the repeating of the following string of words :

'St. Peter, sitting on a marble stone, our Saviour passing by, asked him what was the matter. "Oh, Lord, a toothache!" "Stand up, Peter, and follow me; and whoever keeps these words in memory of me shall never be troubled with a toothache. Amen."'

The English astrologer, Lilly, after the death of his wife, formerly a Mrs. Wright, found in a scarlet bag which she wore under her arm, a pure gold 'sigil', or round plate, worth about ten dollars in gold, which the former husband of the defunct had used to exorcise a spirit that plagued him. In case any of my readers can afford bullion enough, and would like to drive away any such visitor, let them get such a plate and have engraved round the edge of one side, 'Vicit Leo de tribus Judæ tetragrammaton +.' Inside this engrave a 'holy lamb'. Round the edge of the other side engrave 'Annaphel', and three crosses, thus : + + +; and in the middle, 'Sanctus Petrus Alpha et Omega.'

The witches have always had incantations, which they have used to make a broomstick into a horse, to kill or to sicken animals and persons, &c. Most of these are sufficiently stupid, and not half so wonderful as one I know, which may be found in a certain mysterious volume, called *The Girl's Own Book*, and which, as I can depose, has often power to tickle children. It is this :

'Bandy-legged Borachio Mustachio Whiskerifusticus, the bald and brave Bombardino of Bagdad, helped Abomilique Bluebeard Bashaw of Babelmandel beat down an abominable bumblebee at Balsora.'

But to the other witches. Their charms were repeated sometimes in their own language and sometimes in gibberish. When the Scottish witches wanted to fly away to their 'Witches' Sabbath', they straddled a broom-handle, a corn-stalk, a straw, or a rush, and cried out, 'Horse and hattock, in the devil's name !' and immediately away they flew, 'forty times as high as the moon,' if they wished. Some English witches in Somerset used instead to say, 'Thout, tout, throughout, and about;' and when they wished to return from their meeting, they said, 'Rentum, tormentum!' If this form of the charm does not manufacture a horse, or even a saw-horse, then I recommend another version of it, thus:

> *'Horse and pattock, horse and go!*
> *Horse and pellats, ho, ho, ho!'*

German witches said (in High Dutch):

> *'Up and away!*
> *Hi! Up aloft, and nowhere stay!'*

Scottish witches had modes of working destruction to the persons or property of those to whom they meant evil, which were strikingly like the negro obeah or mandinga. One of these was, to make a hash of the flesh of an unbaptized child, with that of dogs and sheep, and to put this goodly dish in the house of the victim, reciting the following rhyme:

> *'We put this until this hame*
> *In our Lord the Devil's name;*
> *The first hands that handle thee,*
> *Burned and scalded may they be!*
> *We will destroy houses and hald,*
> *With the sheep and not (i.e. cattle) into the fauld;*
> *And little shall come to the fore (i.e. remain),*
> *Of all the rest of the little store.'*

Another, used to destroy the sons of a certain gentleman named Gordon was, to make images for the boys, of clay and paste, and put them in a fire, saying:

> *'We put this water among this meal*
> *For long pining and ill heal,*
> *We put it into the fire*
> *To burn them up stook and stour (i.e. stack and band).*
> *That they be burned with our will,*
> *Like any stikkle (stubble) in a kiln.'*

In case any lady reader finds herself changed into a hare, let her remember how the witch Isobel Gowdie changed herself from hare back to woman. It was by repeating:

> 'Hare, hare, God send thee cure!
> I am in a hare's likeness now;
> But I shall be woman even now—
> Hare, hare, God send thee care!'

About the year 1600 there was both hanged and burned at Amsterdam a poor demented Dutch girl, who alleged that she could make the cattle sterile, and bewitch pigs and poultry by saying to them, 'Turius und Shurius Inturius.' I recommend to say this first to an old hen, and if found useful, it might then be tried on a pig.

Not far from the same time a woman was executed as a witch at Bamberg, having, as was often the case, been forced by torture to make a confession. She said that the devil had given her power to send diseases upon those she hated, by saying complimentary things about them, as 'What a strong man!' 'What a beautiful woman!' 'What a sweet child!' It is my own impression that this species of cursing may safely be tried where it does not include a falsehood.

Here are two charms which the German witches used to repeat to raise the devil within the form of a he goat:

> 'Lalle, Bachea, Magotte, Baphia, Dajam,
> Vagoth Heneche Ammi Nagaz, Adomator
> Raphael Immanuel Christus Tetragrammaton
> Agra Jod Loi. Konig! Konig!'

The two last words to be screamed out quickly. This second one, it must be remembered, is to be read backward except the two last words. It was supposed to be the strongest of all, and was used if the first one failed:

> 'Anion, Lalle, Sabolos, Sado, Poter, Aziel,
> Adonai Sado Vagoth Agra, Jod,
> Baphra! Komm! Komm!'

Just in case the devil stayed too long, he could be made to take himself off by addressing to him the following statement, repeated backward:

> 'Zellianelle Heotti Bonus Vagotha
> Plisos sother osech unicus Beelzebub
> Dax! Komm! Komm!'

Which would evidently make almost anybody go away.

A German charm to improve one's finances was perhaps no worse than gambling in gold. It ran thus :

> *'As God be welcomed, gentle moon—*
> *Make thou my money more and soon!'*

To get rid of a fever in the German manner, go and tie up a bough of a tree, saying, 'Twig, I bind thee; fever, now leave me !' To give your ague to a willow tree, tie three knots in a branch of it early in the morning, and say, 'Good morning, old one ! I give thee the cold; good morning, old one !' and turn and run away as fast as you can without looking back.

Enough of this nonsense. It is pure mummery. Yet it is worth while to know exactly what the means were which in ancient times were relied on for such purposes, and it is not useless to put this matter on record; for just such formulas are believed in now by many people. Even in this city there are 'witches', who humbug the more foolish part of the community out of their money by means just as foolish as these.

THE TRYALS OF THE NEW ENGLAND WITCHES

Cotton Mather

Here were in Salem, June 10, 1692, about 40 persons that were afflicted with horrible torments by *Evil Spirits*; and the afflicted have accused 60 or 70 as witches, for that they have *Spectral appearances* of them though the Persons are absent when they are tormented. When these Witches were Tryed, several of them confessed a contract with the Devil, by signing his Book, and did express much sorrow for the same, declaring also their *Confederate Witches*, and said the Tempters of them desired them to sign the *Devils Book*, who tormented them till they did it. There were at the time of Examination, before many hundreds of Witnesses, strange Pranks play'd; such as the taking Pins out of the Clothes of the afflicted, and thrusting them into their flesh, many of which were taken out again by the Judges own hands. Thorns also in like kind were thrust into their flesh; the accusers were sometimes *struck dumb, deaf, blind*, and sometimes lay as if they were dead for a while, and all foreseen and declared by the afflicted just before it was done. Of the afflicted there were two Girls, about 12 or 13 years of age, who saw all that was done, and were therefore called the *Visionary Girls*; for these Girls, and others of the afflicted, say, *they see Coffins, and bodies in Shrouds*, rising up, and looking on the accused, crying, *Vengeance, Vengeance on the Murderers*. Many other strange things were transacted before the Court in the time of their Examination; and especially one thing which I had like to have forgot, which is this. One of the accus'd, whilst the rest were under Examination, was drawn up by a Rope to the Roof of the house where he was, and would have been choak'd in all probability, had not the Rope been presently cut; the Rope hung at the Roof by some *invisible type*, for there was no hole where it went up; but after it was cut the remainder of it was found in the Chamber just above, lying by the very place where it hung down.

In December 1692, the Court sat again at Salem in New England, and cleared about 40 persons suspected for

Witches, and Condemned three. The Evidence against these three was the same as formerly, so the Warrant for their Execution was sent, and the *Graves digged* for the said three, and for about five more that had been Condemned at Salem formerly, but were Reprieved by the Governor.

THE SALEM MASS

Nathaniel Hawthorne

Young Goodman Brown came forth at sunset into the street of Salem village; but put his head back, after crossing the threshold, to exchange a parting kiss with his young wife. And Faith, as the wife was aptly named, thrust her own pretty head into the street, letting the wind play with the pink ribbons of her cap while she called to Goodman Brown.

'Dearest heart,' whispered she, softly and rather sadly, when her lips were close to his ear, 'prithee put off your journey until sunrise and sleep in your own bed tonight. A lone woman is troubled with such dreams and such thoughts that she's afeared of herself sometimes. Pray tarry with me this night, dear husband, of all nights in the year.'

'My love and my Faith,' replied young Goodman Brown, 'of all nights in the year, this one night must I tarry away from thee. My journey, as thou callest it, forth and back again, must needs be done 'twixt now and sunrise. What, my sweet, pretty wife, dost thou doubt me already, and we but three months married?'

'Then God bless you!' said Faith, with pink ribbons; 'and may you find all well when you come back.'

'Amen!' cried Goodman Brown. 'Say thy prayers, dear Faith, and go to bed at dusk, and no harm will come to thee.'

So they parted; and the young man pursued his way until, being about to turn the corner by the meeting-house, he looked back and saw the head of Faith still peeping after him with a melancholy air, in spite of her pink ribbons.

'Poor little Faith!' thought he, for his heart smote him. 'What a wretch am I to leave her on such an errand! She talks of dreams, too. Methought as she spoke, there was trouble in her face, as if a dream had warned her what work is to be done tonight. But no, no; 'twould kill her to think it. Well, she's a blessed angel on earth; and after this one night I'll cling to her skirts and follow her to heaven.'

With this excellent resolve for the future, Goodman Brown felt himself justified in making more haste on his present evil purpose. He had taken a dreary road, darkened by all the gloomiest trees of the forest, which barely stood aside to let the narrow path creep through, and closed immediately behind. It was all as lonely as could be; and there is this peculiarity in such a solitude, that the traveller knows not who may be concealed by the innumerable trunks and the thick boughs overhead; so that with lonely footsteps he may yet be passing through an unseen multitude.

'There may be a devilish Indian behind every tree,' said Goodman Brown to himself; and he glanced fearfully behind him as he added, 'What if the Devil himself should be at my very elbow!'

His head being turned back, he passed a crook of the road, and, looking forward again, beheld the figure of a man, in grave and decent attire, seated at the foot of an old tree. He arose at Goodman Brown's approach and walked onward side by side with him.

'You are late, Goodman Brown,' said he. 'The clock of the Old South was striking as I came through Boston; and that is full fifteen minutes agone.'

'Faith kept me back awhile,' replied the young man, with a tremor in his voice, caused by the sudden appearance of his companion, though not wholly unexpected.

It was now deep dusk in the forest, and deepest in that part of it where these two were journeying. As nearly as could be discerned, the second traveller was about fifty years old, apparently in the same rank of life as Goodman Brown, and bearing a considerable resemblance to him, though perhaps more in expression than features. Still they might have been taken for father and son. And yet, though the elder person was as simply clad as the younger and as simple in manner too, he had an indescribable air of one who knew the world, and who would not have felt abashed at the governor's dinner-table or in King William's court, were it possible that his affairs should call him thither. But the only thing about him that could be fixed upon as remarkable was his staff, which bore the likeness of a great black snake, so curiously wrought that it might almost be seen to twist and wriggle itself like a living serpent. This, of course, must have been an ocular deception, assisted by the uncertain light.

'Come, Goodman Brown,' cried his fellow-traveller, 'this is a dull place for the beginning of a journey. Take my staff, if you are so soon weary.'

'Friend,' said the other, exchanging his slow pace for a full stop, 'having kept covenant by meeting thee here, it is my purpose now to return whence I came. I have scruples touching the matter thou wot'st of.'

'Sayest thou so?' replied he of the serpent, smiling apart. 'Let us walk on, nevertheless, reasoning as we go; and if I convince thee not, thou shalt turn back. We are but a little way in the forest yet.'

'Too far! too far!' exclaimed the good man, unconsciously resuming his walk. 'My father never went into the woods on such an errand, nor his father before him. We have been a race of honest men and good Christians since the days of the martyrs; and shall I be the first by the name of Brown that ever took this path and kept—'

'Such company, thou wouldn't say,' observed the elder person, interpreting his pause. 'Well said, Goodman Brown! I have been as well acquainted with your family as with ever a one among the Puritans; and that's no trifle to say. I helped your grandfather, the constable, when he lashed the Quaker woman so smartly through the streets of Salem; and it was I that brought your father a pitch-pine knot, kindled at my own hearth, to set fire to an Indian village, in King Philip's war. They were my good friends both; and many a pleasant walk have we had along this path, and returned merrily after midnight. I would fain be friends with you for their sake.'

'If it be as thou sayest,' replied Goodman Brown, 'I marvel they never spoke of these matters; or, verily, I marvel not, seeing that the least rumour of the sort would have driven them from New England. We are a people of prayer, and good works to boot, and abide no such wickedness.'

'Wickedness or not,' said the traveller with the twisted staff, 'I have a very general acquaintance here in New England. The deacons of divers towns make me their chairman; and a majority of the Great and General Court are firm supporters of my interests. The governor and I, too – these are state secrets.'

'Can this be so?' cried Goodman Brown, with a stare of amazement at his undisturbed companion. 'Howbeit, I have nothing to do with the governor and council; they have their own ways, and are no rule for a simple husbandman like me. But, were I to go on with thee, how should I meet the eye of that good old man, our minister, at Salem village? Oh, his voice would make me tremble both Sabbath day and lecture day!'

Thus far the elder traveller had listened with due gravity; but now burst into a fit of irrepressible mirth, shaking himself so violently that his snake-like staff actually seemed to wriggle in sympathy.

'Ha! ha! ha!' shouted he again and again; then composing himself, 'Well, go on, Goodman Brown, go on; but, prithee, don't kill me with laughing.'

'Well, then, to end the matter at once,' said Goodman Brown, considerably nettled, 'there is my wife, Faith. It would break her dear little heart, and I'd rather break my own.'

'Nay, if that be the case,' answered the other, 'e'en go thy ways, Goodman Brown. I would not for twenty old women like the one hobbling before us that Faith should come to any harm.'

As he spoke, he pointed his staff at a female figure on the path, in whom Goodman Brown recognized a very pious and exemplary dame, who had taught him catechism in youth, and was still his moral and spiritual adviser, jointly with the minister and Deacon Gookin.

'A marvel, truly, that Goody Cloyse should be so far in the wilderness at nightfall,' said he. 'But, with your leave, friend, I shall take a cut through the woods until we have left this Christian woman behind. Being a stranger to you, she might ask whom I was consorting with and whither I was going.'

'Be it so,' said his fellow-traveller. 'Betake you to the woods, and let me keep the path.'

Accordingly the young man turned aside, but took care to watch his companion, who advanced softly along the road until he had come within a staff's length of the old dame. She, meanwhile, was making the best of her way, with singular speed for so aged a woman, and mumbling some indistinct words – a prayer, doubtless – as she went. The traveller put forth his staff and touched her withered neck with what seemed the serpent's tail.

'The Devil!' screamed the pious old lady.

'Then Goody Cloyse knows her old friend?' observed the traveller, confronting her and leaning on his writhing stick.

'Ah, forsooth, and is it your worship indeed?' cried the good old dame. 'Yea, truly is it, and in the very image of my old gossip, Goodman Brown, the grandfather of the silly fellow that now is. But – would your worship believe it? – my broomstick hath strangely disappeared, stolen as I suspect, by that unhanged witch, Goody Cory, and that, too, when I was all anointed with the juice of smallage, and cinquefoil, and wolf's-bane—'

'Mingled with fine wheat and the fat of a new-born babe,' said the shape of old Goodman Brown.

'Ah, your worship knows the recipe,' cried the old lady, cackling aloud. 'So, as I was saying, being all ready for the meeting, and no horse to ride on, I made up my mind to foot it; for they tell me there is a nice young man to be taken into communion tonight. But now your good worship will lend me your arm, and we shall be there in a twinkling.'

'That can hardly be,' answered her friend. 'I may not spare you my arm, Goody Cloyse; but here is my staff, if you will.'

So saying, he threw it down at her feet, where, perhaps, it assumed life, being one of the rods which its owner had formerly lent to the Egyptian magi. Of this fact, however, Goodman Brown could not take cognizance. He had cast up his eyes in astonishment, and looking down again, beheld neither Goody Cloyse nor the serpentine staff, but his fellow-traveller alone, who waited for him as calmly as if nothing had happened.

'That old woman taught me my catechism,' said the young man; and there is a world of meaning in this simple comment.

They continued to walk onward, while the elder traveller exhorted his companion to make good speed and persevere in the path, discoursing so aptly that his arguments seemed rather to spring up in the bosom of his auditor than to be suggested by himself. As they went, he plucked a branch of maple to serve for a walking-stick, and began to strip it of the twigs and little boughs, which were wet with evening dew. The moment his fingers touched them they became strangely withered and dried up as with a week's sunshine. Thus the pair proceeded, at a good free pace, until suddenly, in a gloomy hollow of the road Goodman Brown sat himself down on the stump of a tree and refused to go any farther.

'Friend,' said he, stubbornly, 'my mind is made up. Not another step will I budge on this errand. What if a wretched old woman do choose to go to the Devil when I thought she was going to heaven : is that any reason why I should quit my dear Faith and go after her?'

'You will think better of this by and by,' said his acquaintance, composedly. 'Sit here and rest yourself awhile; and when you feel like moving again, there's my staff to help you along.'

Without more words, he threw his companion the maple stick, and was as speedily out of sight as if he had vanished into the deepening gloom. The young man sat a few moments by the roadside, applauding himself greatly and thinking with how clear a conscience he should meet the minister in his morning walk, nor shrink from the eye of good old Deacon Gookin. And what calm sleep would be his that very night, which was to have been spent so wickedly, but so purely and sweetly now, in the arms of Faith ! Amidst these pleasant and praiseworthy meditations, Goodman Brown heard the tramp of horses along the road, and deemed it advisable to conceal himself within the verge of the forest, conscious of the guilty purpose that had brought him thither, though now so happily turned from it.

On came the hoof-tramps and the voices of the riders, two grave old voices, conversing soberly as they drew near. These mingled sounds appeared to pass along the road, within a few yards of the young man's hiding-place; but, owing doubtless to the depth of the gloom at that particular spot, neither the travellers nor their steeds were visible. Though their figures brushed the small boughs by the wayside, it could not be seen that they intercepted, even for a moment, the faint gleam from the strip of bright sky athwart which they must have passed. Goodman Brown alternately crouched and stood on tiptoe, pulling aside the branches and thrusting forth his head as far as he durst, without discerning so much as a shadow. It vexed him the more, because he could have sworn, were such a thing possible, that he recognized the voices of the minister and Deacon Gookin, jogging along quietly, as they were wont to do, when bound to some ordination or ecclesiastical council. While yet within hearing, one of the riders stopped to pluck a switch.

'Of the two, reverend sir,' said the voice like the deacon's, 'I had rather miss an ordination dinner than tonight's meeting. They tell me that some of our community are to be here from Falmouth and beyond, and others from Connecticut and Rhode Island, besides several of the Indian pow-wows, who, after their fashion, know almost as much devilry as the best of us. Moreover, there is a goodly young woman to be taken into communion.'

'Mighty well, Deacon Gookin!' replied the solemn old tones of the minister. 'Spur up, or we shall be late. Nothing can be done, you know, until I get on the ground.'

The hoofs clattered again; and the voices, talking so strangely in the empty air, passed on through the forest, where no church had ever been gathered or solitary Christian prayed. Whither, then, could these holy men be journeying so deep into the heathen wilderness? Young Goodman Brown caught hold of a tree for support, being ready to sink down on the ground, faint and overburdened with the heavy sickness of his heart. He looked up to the sky, doubting whether there really was a heaven above him. Yet there was the blue arch, and the stars brightening in it.

'With heaven above and Faith below, I will yet stand firm against the Devil!' cried Goodman Brown.

While he still gazed upward into the deep arch of the firmament and had lifted his hands to pray, a cloud, though no wind was stirring, hurried across the zenith and hid the brightening stars. The blue sky was still visible except directly overhead, where this black mass of cloud was sweeping swiftly northward. Aloft in the air, as if from the depths of the cloud, came a confused and doubtful sound of voices. Once the listener fancied that he could distinguish the accents of townspeople of his own, men and women, both pious and ungodly, many of whom he had met at the communion-table, and had seen others rioting at the tavern. The next moment, so indistinct were the sounds, he doubted whether he had heard aught but the murmur of the old forest, whispering without a wind. Then came a stronger swell of those familiar tones, heard daily in the sunshine at Salem village, but never until now from a cloud of night. There was one voice, of a young woman, uttering lamentations, yet with an uncertain sorrow, and entreating for some favour, which, perhaps, it would grieve her to obtain; and all the unseen multitudes, both saints and sinners, seemed to encourage her onward.

'Faith!' shouted Goodman Brown, in a voice of agony and desperation; and the echoes of the forest mocked him, crying,

'Faith! Faith!' as if bewildered wretches were seeking her all through the wilderness.

The cry of grief, rage and terror was yet piercing the night, when the unhappy husband held his breath for a response. There was a scream, drowned immediately in a louder murmur of voices, fading into far-off laughter, as the dark cloud swept away, leaving the clear and silent sky above Goodman Brown. But something fluttered lightly down through the air and caught on the branch of a tree. The young man seized it, and beheld a pink ribbon.

'My Faith is gone!' cried he, after one stupefied moment. 'There is no good on earth; and sin is but a name. Come, Devil; for to thee is this world given.'

And, maddened with despair, so that he laughed aloud and long, did Goodman Brown grasp his staff and set forth again, at such a rate that he seemed to fly along the forest path rather than to walk or run. The road grew wilder and drearier and more faintly traced, and vanished at length, leaving him in the heart of the dark wilderness, still rushing onward with the instinct that guides mortal man to evil. The whole forest was peopled with frightful sounds – the creaking of the trees, the howling of wild beasts, and the yell of Indians; while sometimes the wind tolled like a distant church-bell, and sometimes gave a broad roar around the traveller, as if all Nature were laughing him to scorn. But he was himself the chief horror of the scene, and shrank not from its other horrors.

'Ha! ha! ha!' roared Goodman Brown when the wind laughed at him. 'Let us hear which will laugh loudest. Think not to frighten me with your devilry. Come witch, come wizard, come Indian pow-wow, come Devil himself, and here comes Goodman Brown. You may as well fear him as he fear you.'

In truth, all through the haunted forest there could be nothing more frightful than the figure of Goodman Brown. On he flew among the black pines, brandishing his staff with frenzied gestures, now giving vent to an inspiration of horrid blasphemy, and now shouting forth such laughter as set all the echoes of the forest laughing like demons around him. The fiend in his own shape is less hideous than when he rages in the breast of man. Thus sped the demoniac on his course, until, quivering among the trees, he saw a red light before him, as when the felled trunks and branches of a clearing have been set on fire, and throw up their lurid blaze against the sky, at the hour of midnight. He paused, in a lull of the tempest that had driven him onward, and heard the swell of what seemed a hymn rolling solemnly from a distance with the weight of many voices. He knew the tune; it was a familiar one in the choir of the village meeting-house. The verse died heavily away, and was lengthened by a chorus, not of human voices, but of all the sounds of the benighted wilderness pealing in awful harmony together. Goodman Brown cried out; and his cry was lost to his own ear by its unison with the cry of the desert.

In the interval of silence he stole forward until the light glared full upon his eyes. At one extremity of an open space, hemmed in by the dark wall of the forest, arose a rock, bearing some rude, natural resemblance either to an altar or a pulpit and surrounded by four blazing pines, their tops aflame, their stems untouched, like candles at an evening meeting. The mass of foliage that had overgrown the summit of the rock was all on fire, blazing high into the night and fitfully illuminating the whole field. Each pendent twig and leafy festoon was in a blaze. As the red light arose and fell, a numerous congregation alternately shone forth, then disappeared in shadow, and again grew, as it were, out of the darkness, peopling the heart of the solitary woods at once.

'A grave and dark-clad company,' quoth Goodman Brown. In truth they were such. Among them, quivering to and fro between gloom and splendour, appeared faces that would be seen next day at the council board of the province, and others which, Sabbath after Sabbath, looked devoutly heavenward, and benignantly over the crowded pews, from the holiest pulpits in the land. Some affirmed that the lady of the governor was there. At least there were high dames well known to her, and wives of honoured husbands, and widows, a great multitude, and ancient maidens, all of excellent repute, and fair young girls, who trembled lest their mothers should espy them. Either the sudden gleams of light flashing over the obscure field bedazzled Goodman Brown, or he recognized a score of the church members of Salem village famous for their especial sanctity. Good old Deacon Gookin had arrived, and waited at the skirts of that venerable saint, his reverend pastor. But, irreverently consorting with these grave, reputable, and pious people, these elders of the church, these chaste dames and dewy virgins, there were men of dissolute lives and women of spotted fame, wretches given over to all mean and filthy vice, and suspected even of horrid crimes. It was strange to see that the good shrank not from the wicked, nor were the sinners abashed by the saints. Scattered also among their pale-faced enemies were the Indian priests, or pow-wows, who had often scared their native forest with more hideous incantations than any known to English witchcraft.

'But where is Faith?' thought Goodman Brown; and, as hope came into his heart, he trembled.

Another verse of the hymn arose, a slow and mournful strain, such as the pious love, but joined to words which expressed all that our nature can conceive of sin, and darkly hinted at far more. Unfathomable to mere mortals is the lore of fiends. Verse after verse was sung; and still the chorus of the desert swelled between like the deepest tone of a mighty organ; and with the final peal of that dreadful anthem there came a sound, as if the roaring wind, the rushing streams, the howling beasts, and every other voice of the unconverted wilderness were mingling and according with the voice of guilty man in homage to the prince of all. The four blazing pines threw up a loftier flame, and obscurely discovered shapes and visages of horror on the smoke wreaths above the impious assembly. At the same moment the fire on the rock shot redly forth and formed a glowing arch above its base, where now appeared a figure. With reverence be it spoken, the figure bore no slight similitude, both in garb and manner, to some grave divine of the New England churches.

'Bring forth the converts!' cried a voice that echoed through the field and rolled into the forest.

At the word, Goodman Brown stepped forth from the shadow of the trees and approached the congregation, with whom he felt a loathful brotherhood by the sympathy of all that was wicked in his heart. He could have wellnigh sworn that the shape of his own dead father beckoned him to advance, looking downward from a smoke-wreath, while a woman, with dim features of despair, threw out her hand to warn him back. Was it his mother? But he had no power to retreat one step, nor to resist, even in thought, when the minister and good old Deacon Gookin seized his arms and led him to the blazing rock. Thither came also the slender form of a veiled female, led between Goody Cloyse, that pious teacher of the catechism, and Martha Carrier, who had received the Devil's promise to be queen of hell. A rampant hag was she. And there stood the proselytes beneath the canopy of fire.

'Welcome my children,' said the dark figure, 'to the communion of your race. Ye have found thus young your nature and your destiny. My children, look behind you!'

They turned; and flashing forth, as it were, in a sheet of flame, the fiend worshippers were seen; the smile of welcome gleamed darkly on every visage.

'There,' resumed the sable form, 'are all whom ye have reverenced from youth. Ye deemed them holier than yourselves, and shrank from your own sin, contrasting it with their lives of righteousness and prayerful aspirations heavenwards. Yet here are they all in my worshipping assembly. This night it shall be granted to you to know their secret deeds; how hoary-bearded elders of the church have whispered wanton words to the young maids of their households; how many a woman, eager for widow's weeds, has given her husband a drink at bedtime and let him sleep his last sleep in her bosom; how beardless youths have made haste to inherit their father's wealth; and how fair damsels – blush not, sweet ones – have dug little graves in the garden and bidden me, the sole guest, to an infant's funeral. By the sympathy of your human hearts for sin ye shall scent out all the places – whether in church, bed-chamber, street, field or forest – where crime has been committed, and shall exult to behold the whole earth one stain of guilt, one mighty blood-spot. Far more than this. It shall be yours to penetrate, in every bosom, the deep mystery of sin, the fountain of all wicked arts, and which inexhaustibly supplies more evil impulses than human power – than my power at its utmost – can make manifest in deeds. And now, my children, look upon each other.'

They did so; and, by the blaze of the hell-kindled torches, the wretched man beheld his Faith, and the wife her husband, trembling before that unhallowed altar.

'Lo, there ye stand, my children,' said the figure, in a deep and solemn tone, almost sad with its despairing awfulness, as if his once angelic nature could yet mourn for our miserable race. 'Depending upon one another's hearts, ye had still hoped that virtue were not all a dream. Now are ye un-

71

deceived. Evil is the nature of mankind. Evil must be your only happiness. Welcome again, my children, to the communion of your race.'

'Welcome,' repeated the fiend worshippers, in one cry of despair and triumph.

And there they stood, the only pair, as it seemed, who were yet hesitating on the verge of wickedness in this dark world. A basin was hollowed, naturally, in the rock. Did it contain water, reddened by the lurid light? or was it blood? or, perchance, a liquid flame? Herein did the shape of evil dip his hand and prepare to lay the mark of baptism upon their foreheads, that they might be partakers of the mystery of sin, more conscious of the secret guilt of others, both in deed and thought than they could now be of their own. The husband cast one look at his pale wife, and Faith at him. What polluted wretches would the next glance show them to each other, shuddering alike at what they disclosed and what they saw!

'Faith! Faith!' cried the husband, 'look up to Heaven, and resist the wicked one.'

Whether Faith obeyed, he knew not. Hardly had he spoken, when he found himself amid calm night and solitude, listening to a roar of the wind which died heavily away through the forest. He staggered against the rock, and felt it chill and damp; while a hanging twig, that had been all on fire, besprinkled his cheek with the coldest dew.

The next morning young Goodman Brown came slowly into the street of Salem village, staring around him like a bewildered man. The good old minister was taking a walk along the graveyard to get an appetite for breakfast and meditate his sermon and bestowed a blessing, as he passed, on Goodman Brown. He shrank from the venerable saint as if to avoid an anathema. Old Deacon Gookin was at domestic worship, and the holy words of his prayer were heard through the open window. 'What God doth the wizard pray to?' quoth Goodman Brown. Goody Cloyse, that excellent old Christian, stood in the early sunshine at her own lattice, catechizing a little girl who had brought her a pint of morning's milk. Goodman Brown snatched away the child as from the grasp of the fiend himself. Turning the corner by the meeting-house, he spied the head of Faith, with the pink ribbons, gazing anxiously forth, and bursting into such joy at sight of him that she skipped along the street and almost kissed her husband before the whole village. But Goodman Brown looked sternly and sadly into her face, and passed on without a greeting.

Had Goodman Brown fallen asleep in the forest, and only dreamed a wild dream of a witch-meeting?

Be it so, if you will; but, alas! it was a dream of evil omen for young Goodman Brown. A stern, a sad, a darkly meditative, a distrustful, if not a desperate, man did he become from the night of that fearful dream. On the Sabbath day, when the congregation were singing a holy psalm, he could not listen, because the anthem of sin rushed loudly upon his ear and drowned all the blessed strain. When the minister spoke from the pulpit, with power and fervid eloquence, and with his hand on the open Bible, of the sacred truths of our religion, and of saint-like lives and triumphant deaths, and of future bliss or misery unutterable, then did Goodman Brown turn pale, dreading lest the roof should thunder down upon the grey blasphemer and his hearers. Often, awakening at midnight, he shrank from the bosom of Faith; and at morning or eventide, when the family knelt down to prayer, he scowled, and muttered to himself, and gazed sternly at his wife, and turned away. And when he had lived long, and was borne to his grave, a hoary corpse, followed by Faith, an aged woman, and children and grand-children, a goodly procession, besides neighbours not a few, they carved no hopeful verse upon his tombstone; for his dying hour was gloom.

THE BLACK LODGE

Aleister Crowley

The Operation planned by the Black Lodge was simple and colossal both in theory and in practice. It was based on the prime principle of Sympathetic Magic, which is that if you destroy anything which is bound up with anybody by an identifying link that person also perishes. Douglas had adroitly taken advantage of the fact of the analogy between his own domestic situation and that of Cyril Grey. He had no need to attack the young magician directly, or even his wife, Lisa; he had merely to conduct the required ritual and this would undoubtedly bring about the downfall of his enemy. For if he could bring Cyril's magic to naught, that exorcist would be destroyed by the recoil of his own exorcism. The laws of force take no account of human prejudices about 'good' or 'evil'; if one is run over by a railway engine, it matters nothing, physically, whether one is trying to commit suicide or to save a child. The difference in the result lies wholly on a superior plane.

For great operations – the 'set pieces' of his diabolical pyrotechnics – Douglas had a place set apart and prepared. This was an old wine-cellar in a street between the Seine and the Boulevard St. Germain. The entrance was comparatively reputable, being a house of cheap prostitution which he and one of his associates, Balloch – screened behind a woman – owned between them. Below this house was a cellar where the appaches of Paris gathered to dance and plot against society; so ran the legend, and two burly *sergents de ville*, with fixed bayonets and cocked revolvers lying on the table before them, superintended the revels. For in fact Douglas had perceived that the apache spent no money, and that it would pay better to run the cellar as a show place for Americans, Englishmen, Germans, and country cousins from the provinces on a jaunt to Paris, on the hunt for thrills. No one more dangerous than a greengrocer had crossed that threshold for many a long year, and the visible apaches, drinking and swearing, dancing an alleged can-can and occasionally throwing bottles and knives at each other, were honest folk painfully earning the exiguous salary which the 'long firm' paid them.

But beneath this cellar, unknown even to the police, was a vault which had once served for storing spirits. It was below the level of the river; rats, damp, and stale alcohol gave it an atmosphere happily peculiar to such abodes. There is no place in the world more law-abiding than a house of ill-fame, with the light of police supervision constantly upon it; and the astuteness of the sorcerer in choosing this for his place of evocation was rewarded by complete freedom from disturbance or suspicion. Anyone could enter at any hour of day or night, with every precaution of secrecy, without drawing more than a laugh from the police on guard.

The entrance to the sorcerer's den was similarly concealed – by cunning, not by more obvious methods.

A sort of cupboard-shelf, reached by a ladder from the dancing cellar and by a few steps from one of the bedrooms in the house above, was called 'Troppman's refuge', it being said that that celebrated murderer once had lain concealed there for some days. His autograph, and some bad verses (all contributed by an ingenious cabaret singer) were shown upon the walls. It was therefore quite natural and unsuspicious for any visitor to climb up into that room, which was so small that it would only hold one man of average size. His non-reappearance would not cause surprise; he might have gone out the other way; in fact, he would naturally do so. But in the moment of his finding himself alone, he could, if he knew the secret, press a hidden lever which caused the floor to decend bodily. Arrived below, a corridor with three right-angled turns – this could, incidentally, be flooded at need in a few moments – led to the last of the defences, a regular door such as is fitted to a strong-room. There was an emergency exit to the cellar, equally ingenious; it was a sort of torpedo-tube opening beneath the water of the Seine. It was fitted with a compressed air-chamber. Anyone wishing to escape had merely to introduce himself into a shell made of thin cork, and shoot into the river. Even the worst of swimmers could be sure to reach the neighbouring quay. But the secret of this was known only to Douglas and one other.

The very earliest steps in such thoroughgoing sorcery as Douglas practised require the student to deform and mutilate his humanity by accustoming himself to such moral crimes as render their perpetrator callous and insensible to all such

75

emotions as men naturally cherish; in particular, love. The Black Lodge put all its members through regular practices of cruelty and meanness. Guy de Maupassant wrote two of the most revolting stories ever told; one of a boy who hated a horse, the other of a family of peasants who tortured a blind relative that had been left to their charity. Such vileness as is written there by the divine hand of that great artist forbids emulation; the reverent reference must suffice.

Enough to say that stifling of all natural impulse was a preliminary of the system of the Black Lodge; in higher grades the pupil took on the manipulation of subtler forces. Douglas's own use of his wife's love to vitriolize her heart was considered by the best judges as likely to become a classic.

The inner circle, the fourteen men about Douglas himself and that still more mysterious person to whom even he was responsible, a woman known only as 'Annie' or as 'A.B.', were sealed to him by the direst of all bonds. Needless are oaths in the Black Lodge; honour being the first thing discarded, their only use is to frighten fools. But before joining the Fourteen, known as the Ghaaghaael, it was obligatory to commit murder in cold blood, and to place the proof of it in the hands of Douglas. Thus each step in sorcery is also a step in slavery; and that any man should put such power in the hands of another, no matter for what hope of gain, is one of the mysteries of perverse psychology. The highest rank in the Lodge was called Thaumiel-Qeretiel, and there were two of these, 'Annie' and Douglas, who were alone in possession of the full secrets of the Lodge. Only they and the Fourteen had keys to the cellar and the secret of the combination.

Beginners were initiated there, and the method of introducing them was satisfactory and ingenious. They were taken to the house in an automobile, their eyes blinded by an ordinary pair of motor-goggles, behind whose glass was a steel plate.

The cellar itself was arranged as a permanent place of evocation. It was a far more complex device than that used by Vesquit in Naples, for in confusion lay the safety of the Lodge. The floor was covered with symbols which even the Fourteen did not wholly understand; any one of them, crossed inadvertently, might be a magical trap for a traitor; and as each of the Fourteen was exactly that, in fact had to be so to qualify for supreme place, it was with abject fear that this Unholy of Unholies was guarded.

At the appointed hour the Fourteen assembled at the Beth Chol, or House of Horror, as the cellar was called in the jargon of the sorcerers. Among their number were the afore-mentioned Balloch; Cremers, a priest from America; Abdul Bey, a Turk, and Douglas's wife.

The first part of the procedure consisted in the formal renunciation by Mrs. Douglas of the vows taken for her in her baptism, a ceremonial apostacy from Christianity. This was done in no spirit of hostility to that religion, but to permit of her being rebaptized into it under Lisa's maiden name. The Turk was next called upon to renounce Islam, and baptized by the name of the Marchese la Giuffria.

The American priest next proceeded to confirm them in the Christian religion, and to communicate the Sacrament.

Finally, they were married. In this long profanation of the mysteries of the Church the horror lay in the business-like simplicity of the procedure.

One can imagine the Charity of a devout Christian find-ing excuses for the Black Mass, when it is the expression of the revolt of an agonizing soul, or of the hysteria of a half-crazed debauchee; he can conceive of repentance and of grace following upon enlightenment; but this cold-blooded abuse of the most sacred rites, their quite casual employ-ment as the mere prelude to a crime which is tantamount to murder in the opinion of all right-minded men, must seem even to the Freethinker or the Pagan as an abomina-tion not to be forgiven.

No pains had been spared by Douglas to make all secure. Balloch and Cremers had sponsored both 'infants', and Douglas himself, as having most right, gave his wife in marriage to the Turk.

A brutally realistic touch was needed to consummate the sacrilige; it was not neglected.

Much of the pleasure taken by Douglas in this miserable and criminal farce was due to his enjoyment of the suffer-ings of his wife. Each new spurt of filth wrung her heart afresh; and withal she was aware that all these things were but the prelude to an act of fiendish violence more horrible than them all.

Then Cremers and Abdul Bey, their functions ended, were led out of the cellar. Balloch remained to perform the operation from which the bulk of his income was derived.

But there was yet much sorcery of the more secret sort to be accomplished. Douglas who, up to now, had confined himself to intense mental concentration upon the work, forcing himself to believe that the ceremonies he was witnessing were real instead of mockery, that his wife was really Lisa, and Abdul really the Marchese, now came forward as the heart and brain of the work. The difficulty – the crux of the whole art – had been to introduce Cyril Grey into the affair, and this had been overcome by the use of a specimen of his signature. But now it was necessary also to dedicate the victim to Hecate, or rather, to her Hebrew equivalent, Nahema, the devourer of little children, because she also is one aspect of the moon, and Lisa having been adopted to that planet, her representative must needs undergo a similar ensorcelment.

In the art of evocation Douglas was profoundly skilled. His mind was of a material and practical order, and distrusted subtleties. He gladly endured the immense labour of compelling a spirit to visible appearance, when a less careful or more fine-minded sorcerer would have worked upon some other plane. He had so far mastered his art that in a place, such as he now had, long habited to similar scenes, he could call up a visible image of almost any demon required in a period of not more than half an hour. For place-association is of great importance, possibly because it favours concentration of mind. Evidently, it is difficult not to feel religious in King's College Chapel, Cambridge, or otherwise than profoundly sceptical and Pagan in St. Peter's, at Rome, with its 'East' in the West, its adaptation of a statue of Jupiter to represent its patron saint, and the emphasis of its entire architecture in bearing witness that its true name is Temporal Power. Gothic is the only mystic type; Templar and Byzantine are only religious through sexuality; Perpendicular is more moral than spiritual – and modern architecture means nothing at all.

In the Beth Chol there was always a bowl of fresh bull's blood burning over a charcoal brazier.

Science is gradually being forced round once more to the belief that there is something more in life than its mere chemistry and physics. Those who practise the occult arts have never been in doubt on the subject. The dynamic virtue of living substance does not depart from it immediately at death. Those ideas, therefore, which seek manifestation in life, must do so either by incarnation or by seizing some still living matter which the idea or soul in possession has abandoned. Sorcerers consequently employ the fumes of fresh blood as a vehicle for the manifestation of the demons whom they wish to evoke. The matter is easy enough; for fiends are always eager to take hold on the sensory life. Occasionally, such beings find people ignorant and foolish enough to offer themselves deliberately to obsession by sitting in a dark room without magical protection, and inviting any wandering ghost or demon to take hold of them, and use their bodies and minds. This loathsome folly is called Spiritualism, and successful practitioners can be recognized by the fact that their minds are no use for anything at all any more. They become incapable of mental concentration, or a connected train of thought; only too often the obsessing spirit gains power to take hold of them at will, and utters by their mouths foulness and imbecility when the whim takes him. True souls would never seek so ignoble a means of manifesting in earth-life; their ways are holy, and in accord with Nature.

While the true soul reincarnates as a renunciation, a sacrifice of its divine life and ecstasy for the sake of redeeming those who are not yet freed from mortal longings, the demon seeks incarnation as a means of gratifying unslaked lusts.

Like a dumb beast in pain, the wife of Douglas watched her husband go through his ghastly ritual, with averted face, as is prescribed; for none may look on Hecate, and remain sane. The proper conjurations of Hecate are curses against all renewal of life; her sacrament is deadly nightshade or henbane, and her due offering a black lamb torn ere its birth from a black ewe.

This, with sardonic subter-thought, pleasing to Hecate, the sorcerer promised her as she made her presence felt; whether they could have seen anything if they had dared to look, who can say? But through the cellar moved an icy sensation, as if some presence had indeed been called forth by the words and rites spoken and accomplished.

For Hecate is what Scripture calls 'the second death'. Natural death is to man the greatest of the Sacraments, of which all others are but symbols; for it is the final and absolute Union with the creator, and it is also the Pylon of the Temple of Life, even in the material world, for Death is Love.

Certainly the wife of Douglas felt the presence of that vile thing evoked from Tartarus. Its chill struck through to her bones. Nothing had so torn her breast as the constant refusal of her husband to allow her to fulfil her human destiny. Even her prostitution, since it was forced upon her by the one man she loved, might be endured – if only – if only—

But always the aid of Balloch had been summoned; always, in dire distress, and direr danger, she had been thwarted of her life's purpose. It was not so much a conscious wish, though that was strong, as an actual physical craving of her nature, as urgent and devouring as hunger or thirst.

Balloch, who had been all his life high-priest of Hecate, had never been present at an evocation of the force that he served. He shuddered – not a little – as the sorcerer recited his surgical exploits; the credentials of the faith of her servant then present before her. He had committed his dastardly crimes wholly for gain, and as a handle for blackmail; the magical significance of the business had not occurred to him at all. His magical work had been almost entirely directed to the gratification of sensuality in abnormal and extra-human channels. So, while a fierce pride now thrilled him, there was mingled with it a sinking of the spirit; for he realized that its mistress had been sterility and death. And it was of death that he was most afraid. The cynical calm of Douglas appalled him; he recognized the superiority of that great sorcerer; and his hope to supplant him died within his breast.

At that moment Hecate herself passed into him, and twined herself inextricably about his brain. He accepted his destiny as her high-priest; in future he would do murder for the joy of pleasing her! All other mistresses were tame to this one! The thrill of Thuggee caught him – and in a very spasm of maniacal exaltation, he vowed himself again and again to her services. She should be sole goddess of the Black Lodge – only let her show him how to be rid of Douglas! Instantly the plan came to him; he remembered that 'Annie' was high-priestess of Hecate in a greater sense than himself; for she was notorious as an open advocate of this kind of murder; indeed, she had narrowly escaped prison on this charge; he would tempt Douglas to rid himself of 'Annie' – and then betray him to her.

So powerful was the emotion that consumed him that he trembled with excitement and eagerness. Tonight was a great night : it was a step in his initiation to take part in so tremendous a ceremony. He became nervously exalted; he could have danced; Hecate, warming herself in his old bones, communicated a devilish glee to him.

The moment was at hand for his renewed activity.

'Hecate, mother only of death, devourer of all life !' cried Douglas, in his final adjuration; 'as I devote to thy chill tooth this secret spring of man, so be it with all that are like unto it ! Even as it is with that which I shall cast upon thine altar, so be it with all the offspirng of Lisa la Guiffria !'

He ended with the thirteenth repetition of that appalling curse which begins 'ΕΠΙΚΛΛΥΜΑΙ ΚΕ ΤΗΝ ΕΝ ΤΩΙ ΚΕΝΕΩΙ, ΠΝΕΨΜΑΤΙ, ΓΕΙΝΑΝ, ΑΟΡΑΤΑΝ, ΠΑΝΤΟΚΡΑΤΟΡΑ, ΘΕΡΟΠΟΙΑΝ ΚΑΙ ΕΡΗΜΟΠΟΙΑΝ, 'ΗΜΙΚΟΝΤΑ 'ΟΥΚΙΑΝ 'ΕΥΚΤΑΘΟΥΚΑΝ calling upon 'her that dwelleth in the void place, the inane, terrible, inexorable, maker of horror and desolation, hater of the house that prospereth', and devoting 'the signified and sealed, named and unnamed' to destruction.

Then he turned to Balloch, and bade him act. Three minutes later the surgeon gave a curse, and blanched, as a scream, despite herself, burst from the bitten lips of the brave woman who lay upon the altar.

'Why couldn't you let me give an anaesthetic?' he said angrily.

'What's wrong? Is it bad?'

'It's damned ugly. Curse it; not a thing here that I need !'

But he needed nothing; he had done more even than he guessed.

Mrs. Douglas, her face suddenly drawn and white, lifted her head with infinite effort towards her husband.

'I've always loved you,' she whispered, 'and I love you now, as – I – die.'

Her head dropped with a dull crack upon the slab. No one can say if she heard the reply of Douglas :

'You sow ! you've bitched the whole show !'

For she had uttered the supreme name of Love, in love; and the spell dissolved more swiftly than a dream. There was no Hecate, no sorcerer even, for the moment; nothing but two murderers, and the corpse of a martyr between them.

Douglas did not waste a single word of abuse on Balloch. 'This is for you to clear up,' he said, with a simplicity that cut deeper than sneer or snarl, and walked out of the cellar.

Balloch, left to himself, became hysterical. In his act he recognized the first-fruits of the divine possession; his offering to the goddess had been stupendous indeed. All his exaltation returned : now would Hecate favour him above all men !

THE SACRIFICE

Betty May

The ceremony opened with the solemn entrance of the Mystic clad in the gorgeous robes of a Grand Master of the order of Freemasons. After he had seated himself on the throne before the brazier with charcoal fire, around which hung the sacrificial knives and swords, the other members of the cult took their places on the triangular stools at the points of the star. They were dressed as a rule in robes, with the cowls drawn down over their faces, and only their eyes visible through the narrow eye-slits. Clouds of incense hung about the room everywhere. When all were assembled the Mystic rose from his seat, and taking one of the swords from the side of the brazier held it pointing towards the altar while he intoned an invocation in a language with which I was not familiar. From hearing it every day, however, the sounds remain fixed in my memory.

> *'Artay I was Malcooth-Vegabular,*
> *Vegadura, ee-ar-la-ah moov.'*

The last was a high-pitched note in contrast with the rest of the chant. Following this, he walked over to Raoul, rested the point of the sword on his forehead, and uttered a further rigmarole, finishing up with a loud shriek of 'Adonis', which was the name by which my husband was known in the abbey. Then he went through the identical performance in front of Leah, except that to begin with he stood silently in front of her for a full minute, breathing deeply the while – breathing in the soul of his priestess, as it was explained to me afterwards.

These preliminary invocations done, the Mystic proceeded to execute a variety of ecstatic dances. This was both impressive and ludicrous. He lashed himself into an absolute frenzy, brandishing his sword, and dancing and leaping about in the magic circle. His eyes blazed. The words he chanted had a compelling, monotonous and exotic rhythm, and his eyes were alight with fanatical enthusiasm. Every

Friday night there was a special invocation to Pan, in which, as is shown by the hymn for these occasions, the doctrine of the cult became manifest. It was written in English, and I will quote the first few lines,

'Thrill with lissom lust of the light,
    O Man, my Man;
Come careening out of the night
    To me, to me;
Come with Apollo in bridal dress—'

Later we came to the time for the sacrifice and everybody took their accustomed position, except that for this occasion Raoul, as he was to be the executioner, changed places with the Mystic. The stray cat, Mischette, was brought out and placed, still in the sack, on the altar. The air was thick with incense. Raoul recited the invocation, and walked with up-raised sword towards Leah and the others and placed its point on their brows while he uttered the usual formula. I sat outside the magic circle and watched the gruesome performance.

Presently, when much of the ceremony had been gone through, I saw Raoul take a kukri (Gurkha knife) from its place by the brazier and approach the altar, on which was the squirming sack. He untied it, drew forth the struggling and terrified cat, by the scruff of the neck, and held her with his left hand at arm's-length above his head. In his right he held the kukri with its point towards the brazier. The Mystic stilled Mischette's struggles by applying a dab of ether to her nose. All was now ready for the sacrificial invocation, which Raoul had written specially for the occasion, and which he now had to recite in the fatiguing posture that I have described.

It was a long invocation, and before it was half done I could see his left arm quiver with the strain. As he approached the point where the killing was to take place Leah stepped down from her triangular stool, and taking a bowl from the altar, held it underneath Mischette to catch the blood, none of which is supposed to be lost. At last the moment had arrived. I saw him lift back the kukri, and then closed my eyes till it should be over . . . Then, swaying slightly, Raoul laid the carcass on the altar. This done, his resources were exhausted, and the Mystic had to take over the conducting of the ceremony.

Having concluded the invocation, he took the bowl containing the blood, uttered some consecratory formula over it and handed it to Leah, who was standing by. Together they approached Raoul. The Mystic then flung back the cowl from Raoul's face, and dipping a finger in the blood, traced the sign of the Pentagram on his white, glistening forehead, and so to all the others, himself last.

The final rite now alone remained to be performed. The Mystic took a small silver cup, into which he scooped some of the blood from the bowl, and handed it to my husband, who drained it to the dregs. His whole face became deadly white and drawn.

For a time after the ceremony I was convinced that Raoul had been poisoned by the blood of Mischette. But when he got steadily worse and a doctor was summoned I found out that he was suffering from enteritis, a not uncommon disease in those parts. What I did not know was that the disease was to develop complications and these were to lead to the sad death of my beloved, bewildered Raoul . . .

SYLVAN HORRORS

Elliott O'Donnell

I believe trees have spirits; I believe everything that grows
has a spirit, and that such spirits never die, but passing into
another state, a state of film and shadow, live on for ever.
The phantasms of vegetable life are everywhere, though dis-
cernible only to the few of us. Often as I ramble through
thoroughfares, crowded with pedestrians and vehicles, and
impregnated with steam and smoke and all the impurities
arising from over-congested humanity, I have suddenly
smelt a different atmosphere, the cold atmosphere of superphysical forest land. I have come to a halt, and leaning in
some doorway gazed in awestruck wonder at the nodding
foliage of a leviathan lepidodendron, the phantasm of one of
those mammoth lycopods that flourished in the Carboni-
ferous period. I have watched it swaying its shadowy arms
backwards and forwards as if keeping time to some ghostly
music, and the breeze it has thus created has rustled through
my hair, while the sweet scent of its resin has pleasantly
tickled my nostrils. I have seen, too, suddenly open before
me, dark, gloomy aisles, lined with stupendous pines and
carpeted with long, luxuriant grass, gigantic ferns, and other
monstrous primeval flora, of a nomenclature wholly unknown to me; I have watched in chilled fascination the
black trunks twist and bend and contort, as if under the
influence of an uncontrollable fit of laughter, or at the
bidding of some psychic cyclone. I have at times stayed my
steps when in the throes of the city-pavements; shops and
people have been obliterated, and their places taken by
occult foliage; immense fungi have blocked out the sun's
rays, and under the shelter of their slimy, glistening heads, I
have been thrilled to see the wriggling, gliding forms of
countless smaller saprophytes. I have felt the cold touch of
loathsome toadstools and sniffed the hot, dry dust of the
full, ripe puff-ball. On the Thames Embankment, up Chel-
sea way, I have at twilight beheld wonderful metamor-
phoses. In company with the shadows of natural objects of
the landscape, have silently sprung up giant reeds and bull-

rushes. I have felt their icy coldness as, blowing hither and thither in the delirium of their free, untrammelled existence, they have swished across my face. Visions, truly visions, the exquisite fantasies of a vivid imagination. So says the sage. I do not think so; I dispute him *in toto*. These objects I have seen have not been illusions; else, why have I not imagined other things; why, for example, have I not seen rocks walking about and tables coming in at my door? If these phantasms were but tricks of the imagination, then imagination would stop at nothing. But they are not imagination, neither are they the idle fancies of an over-active brain. They are objective – just as much objective as are the smells of recognised physical objects, that those, with keenly sensitive olfactory organs, can detect, and those, with a less sensitive sense of smell, cannot detect; those, with acute hearing, can hear, and those with less acute hearing cannot hear. And yet, people are slow to believe that the seeing of the occult is as much a faculty as is the scenting of smells or the hearing of noises.

I have heard it said that, deep down in coal mines, certain of the workers have seen wondrous sights; that when they have been alone in a drift, they have heard the blowing of the wind and the rustling of leaves, and suddenly found themselves penned in on all sides by the naked trunks of enormous primitive trees, lepidodendrons, sigillarias, ferns, and other plants, that have shone out with phosphorescent grandeur amid the inky blackness of the subterranean ether. Around the feet of the spellbound watchers have sprung up rank blades of Brobdignagian grass and creepers, out of which have crept, with lurid eyes, prodigious millipedes, cockroaches, white ants, myriapods and scorpions, whilst added to the moaning and sighing of the trees has been the humming of stone-flies, dragon-flies, and locusts. Galleries and shafts have echoed and re-echoed with these noises of the old world, which yet lives, and will continue to live, maybe, to the end of time.

But are the physical trees, the trees that we can all see budding and sprouting in our gardens to-day – are they ever cognisant of the presence of the occult? Can they, like certain – not all – dogs and horses and other animals, detect the proximity of the unknown? Do they tremble and shake with fear at the sight of some psychic vegetation, or are they utterly devoid of any such faculty? Can they see, hear, or smell? Have they any senses at all? And, if they have one sense, have they not others? Aye, there is food for reflection.

Personally, I believe trees have senses – not, of course, in such a high state of development as those of animal life; but, nevertheless, senses. Consequently, I think it quite possible that certain of them, like certain animals, feel the presence of the superphysical. I often stroll in woods. I do not love solitude; I love the trees, and I do not think there is anything in nature, apart from man, I love much more. The oak, the ash, the elm, the poplar, the willow, to me are more than mere names; they are friends, the friends of my boyhood and manhood; companions in my lonely rambles and voluntary banishments; guardians of my siestas; comforters of my tribulations. The gentle fanning of their branches has eased my pain-racked brow and given me much-needed sleep, whilst the chlorophyll of their leaves has acted like balm to my eyelids, inflamed after long hours of study. I have leaned my head against their trunks, and heard, or fancied I have heard, the fantastic murmurings of their peaceful minds. This is what happens in the daytime, when the hot summer sun has turned the meadow-grass a golden brown. But with the twilight comes the change. Phantom-land awakes, and mingled with the shadows of the trees and bushes that lazily unroll themselves from trunk and branches are the darkest of shades, that impart to the forest an atmosphere of dreary coldness. Usually I hie away with haste at sunset, but there are occasions when I have dallied longer than I have intended, and only realized my error when it has been too late. I have then, controlled by the irresistible fascination of the woods, waited and watched. I well recollect, for example, being caught in this way in a Hampshire spinney, at that time one of my most frequented haunts. The day had been unusually close and stifling, and the heat, in conjunction with a hard morning's work – for I had written, God only knows how long, without ceasing, – made me frightfully sleepy, and on arriving at my favourite spot beneath a lofty pine, I had slept till, for very shame, my eyelids could keep closed no longer. It was then nine o'clock, and the metamorphosis of sunset had commenced in solemn earnest. The evening was charming, ideal of the heart of summer; the air soft, sweetly scented; the sky unspotted blue. A peaceful hush, broken only by the chiming of some distant church bells, and the faint, the very faint barking of dogs, enveloped everything and instilled in me a false sensation of security. Facing me was a diminutive glade padded with downy grass, transformed into a pale yellow by the lustrous rays of the now encrimsoned sun. Fainter and fainter grew the ruddy glow, until there was nought of it left but a pale pink streak, whose delicate marginal lines still separated the blue of the sky from the quickly superseding grey. A barely perceptible mist gradually cloaked the grass, whilst the gloom amid the foliage on the opposite side of the glade intensified. There was now no sound of bells, no barking of dogs; and silence, a silence tinged with the sadness so characteristic of summer evenings, was everywhere paramount. A sudden rush of icy air made my teeth chatter. I made an effort to stir, to escape ere the grotesque and intangible horrors of the wood could catch me. I ignominiously failed; the soles of my feet froze to the ground. Then I felt the slender, graceful body of the pine against which I leaned my back, shake and quiver, and my hand – the hand that rested on its bark – grew damp and sticky.

I endeavoured to avert my eyes from the open space confronting them. I failed; and as I gazed, filled with the anticipations of the damned, there suddenly burst into view, with all the frightful vividness associated only with the occult, a tall form – armless, legless – fashioned like the gnarled trunk of a tree – white, startlingly white in places where the bark had worn away, but on the whole a bright, a luridly bright, yellow and black. At first I successfully resisted a powerful impulse to raise my eyes to its face; but as I only too well knew would be the case, I was obliged to look at last, and, as I anticipated, I underwent a most violent shock. In lieu of a face I saw a raw and shining polyp, a mass of waving, tossing, pulpy radicles from whose centre shone two long, obliquely set, pale eyes, ablaze with devilry and malice. The thing, after the nature of all terrifying phantasms, was endowed with hypnotic properties, and directly its eyes rested on me I became numb; my muscles slept while my faculties remained awake, acutely awake.

Inch by inch the thing approached me; its stealthy, gliding motion reminding me of a tiger subtly and relentlessly stalking its prey. It came up to me, and the catalepsy which had held me rigidly upright departed. I fell on the ground for protection, and, as the great unknown curved its ghastly figure over me and touched my throat and forehead with its fulsome tentacles, I was overcome with nervous tremors; a deadly pain griped my entrails, and, convulsed with agony, I rolled over on my face, furiously clawing the bracken. In this condition I continued for probably one or even two minutes, though to me it seemed very much longer. My sufferings terminated with the loud report of firearms, and slowly picking myself up, I found that the apparition had vanished, and that standing some twenty or so paces from me was a boy with a gun. I recognized him at once as the son of my neighbour, the village schoolmaster; but not wishing to tarry there any longer, I hurriedly wished him good night, and leaving the copse a great deal more quickly than I had entered it, I hastened home.

What had I seen? A phantasm of some dead tree? some peculiar species of spirit (I have elsewhere termed a vagra-rian), attracted thither by the loneliness of the locality? some vicious, evil phantasm? or a vice-elemental, whose presence there would be due to some particularly wicked crime or series of crimes perpetrated on or near the spot? I cannot say. It might well have been either one of them, or some-thing quite different. I am quite sure, however, that most woods are haunted, and that he who sees spirit phenomena can be pretty certain of seeing them there. Again and again, as I have been passing after nightfall, through tree-girt glen, forest, or avenue, I have seen all sorts of curious forms and shapes move noiselessly from tree to tree. Hooded figures, with death's-heads, have glided surreptitiously through moon-kissed spaces; icy hands have touched me on the shoulders; whilst, pacing alongside me, I have oft-times heard footsteps, light and heavy, though I have seen nothing.

Miss Frances Sinclair tells me that, once, when walking along a country lane, she espied some odd-looking object lying on the ground at the foot of a tree. She approached it, and found to her horror it was a human finger swimming in a pool of blood. She turned round to attract the attention of her friends, and when she looked again the finger had vanished. On this very spot, she was subsequently informed, the murder of a child had taken place.

Trees are, I believe, frequently haunted by spirits that suggest crime. I have no doubt that numbers of people have hanged themselves on the same tree in just the same way as countless people have committed suicide by jumping over certain bridges. Why? For the very simple reason that hovering about these bridges are influences antagonistic to the human race, spirits whose chief and fiendish delight is to breathe thoughts of self-destruction into the brains of passers-by. I once heard of a man, medically pronounced sane, who frequently complained that he was tormented by a voice whispering in his ear, 'Shoot yourself! Shoot yourself!' – advice which he eventually found himself bound to follow. And of a man, likewise stated to be sane, who journeyed a considerable distance to jump over a notorious bridge because he was for ever being haunted by the phantasm of a weirdly beautiful woman who told him to do so. If bridges have their attendant sinister spirits, so undoubtedly have trees – spirits ever anxious to entice within the magnetic circle of their baleful influence anyone of the human race.

Many tales of trees being haunted in this way have come to me from India and the East. I quoted one in my *Ghostly Phenomena*, and the following was told me by a lady whom I met recently, when on a visit to my wife's relations in the Midlands.

'I was riding with my husband along a very lonely mountain road in Assam,' my informant began, 'when I suddenly discovered I had lost my silk scarf, which happened to be a rather costly one. I had a pretty shrewd idea whereabouts I might have dropped it, and, on mentioning the fact to my husband, he at once turned and rode back to look for it. Being armed, I did not feel at all nervous at being left alone, especially as there had been no cases, for many years, of assault on a European in our district; but, seeing a big mango tree standing quite by itself a few yards from the road, I turned my horse's head with the intention of riding up to it and picking some of its fruit. To my great annoyance, however, the beast refused to go; moreover, although at all times most docile, it now reared, and kicked, and showed unmistakable signs of fright.

'I speedily came to the conclusion that my horse was aware of the presence of something – probably a wild beast – I could not see myself, and I at once dismounted, and tethering the shivering animal to a boulder, advanced cautiously, revolver in hand, to the tree. At every step I took, I expected the spring of a panther or some other beast of prey; but, being afraid of nothing but a tiger – and there were none, thank God! in that immediate neighbourhood – I went boldly on. On nearing the tree, I noticed that the soil under the branches was singularly dark, as if scorched and blackened by a fire, and that the atmosphere around it had suddenly grown very cold and dreary. To my disappointment there was no fruit, and I was coming away in disgust, when I caught sight of a queer-looking thing just over my head and half-hidden by the foliage. I parted the leaves asunder with my whip and looked up at it. My blood froze.

'The thing was nothing human. It had a long, grey, nude body, shaped like that of a man, only with abnormally long arms and legs, and very long and crooked fingers. Its head was flat and rectangular, without any features saving a pair of long and heavy lidded, light eyes, that were fixed on mine with an expression of hellish glee. For some seconds I was too appalled even to think, and then the most mad desire to kill myself surged through me. I raised my revolver, and was in the act of placing it to my forehead, when a loud shout from behind startled me. It was my husband. He had found my scarf, and, hurrying back, had arrived just in time to see me raise the revolver – strange to relate – at him! In a few words I explained to him what had happened, and we examined the tree together. But there were no signs of the terrifying phenomenon – it had completely vanished. Though my husband declared that I must have been dreaming, I noticed he looked singularly grave, and, on our return home, he begged me never to go near the tree again. I asked him if he had had any idea it was haunted, and he said: "No! but I know there are such trees. Ask Dingan." Dingan was one of our native servants – the one we respected most, as he had been with my husband for nearly twelve years – ever since, in fact, he had settled in Assam. "The mango tree, mem-sahib!" Dingan exclaimed, when I approached him on the subject, "the mango tree on the Yuka Road, just before you get to the bridge over the river? I know it well. We call it 'the devil tree,' mem-sahib. No other tree will grow near it. There is a spirit peculiar to certain trees that lives in its branches, and persuades anyone who ventures within a few feet of it, either to kill themselves, or to kill other people. I have seen three men from this village alone, hanging to its accursed branches; they were left there till the ropes rotted and the jackals bore them off to the jungles. Three suicides have I seen, and three murders – two were women, strangers in these parts, and they were both lying within the shadow of the mango's trunk, with the backs of their heads broken in like eggs! It is a thrice-accursed tree, mem-sahib." Needless to say, I agreed with Dingan, and in future gave the mango a wide berth.'

Vagrarians, tree devils (a type of vice elemental), and phantasms of dead trees are some of the occult horrors that haunt woods, and, in fact, the whole country-side! Added to these, there are the fauns and satyrs, those queer creatures, undoubtedly vagrarians, half-man and half-goat, that are accredited by the ancients with much merry-making, and grievous to add, much lasciviousness. Of these spirits there is mention in Scripture, namely, Isaiah xiii. 21, where we read : 'And their houses shall be full of doleful creatures, and owls shall dwell there, and satyrs shall dance there'; and in Baddeley's *Historical Meditations*, published about the beginning of the seventeenth century, there is a description by Plutarch, of a satyr captured by Sulla, when the latter was on his way from Dyrrachium to Brindisium. The creature, which appears to have been very material, was found asleep in a park near Apollonia. On being led into the presence of Sulla, it commenced speaking in a harsh voice that was an odd mixture of the neighing of a horse and the crying of a goat. As neither Sulla nor any of his followers could understand in the slightest degree, what the monstrosity meant, they let it go, nor is there any further reference to it.

Now, granted that this account is not 'faked,' and that such a beast actually did exist, it would naturally suggest to one that vagrarians, pixies, and other grotesque forms of phantasms are, after all, only the spirits of similar types of material life, and that, in all probability, the earth, contemporary with prehistoric, and even latter-day man, fairly swarmed with such creatures. However, this, like everything else connected with these early times, is merely a matter of speculation. Another explanatory theory is, that possibly superphysical phenomena were much more common formerly than now, and that the various types of sub-human and sub-animal apparitions (which were then constantly seen by the many, but which are now only visible to the few) have been handed down to us in the likeness of satyrs and fauns. Anyhow, I think they may be rightly classified in the category of vagrarians. The association of spirits with trees is pretty nearly universal. In the fairy tales of youth we have frequent allusions to them. In the Caucasus, where the population is not of Slavonic origin, we have innumerable stories of sacred trees, and in each of these stories the main idea is the same – namely, that a human life is dependent on the existence of a tree. In Slavonic mythology, plants as well as trees are magnets for spirits, and in the sweet-scented pinewoods, in the dark, lonely pinewoods, dwell 'psipolnitza,' or female goblins, who plague the harvesters; and 'lieshi,' or forest male demons, closely allied to satyrs. In Iceland there was a pretty superstition to the effect that, when an innocent person was put to death, a sorb or mountain ash would spring over their grave. In Teutonic mythology the sorb is supposed to take the form of a lily or white rose, and, on the chairs of those about to die, one or other of these flowers is placed by unseen hands. White lilies, too, are emblematic of innocence, and have a knack of mysteriously shooting up on the graves of those who have been unjustly executed. Surely this would be the work of a spirit, as, also, would be the action of the eglantine, which is so charmingly illustrated in the touching story of Tristram and Yseult. Tradition says that from the grave of Tristram there sprang an eglantine which twined about the statue of the lovely Yseult, and, despite the fact of its being thrice cut down, grew again, ever embracing the same fair image. Among the North American Indians there was, and maybe still is, a general belief that the spirits of those who died, naturally reverted to trees – to the great pines of the mountain forests – where they dwelt for ever amid the branches. The Indians believed also that the spirits of certain trees walked at night in the guise of beautiful women. Lucky Indians! Would that my experience of the forest phantasms had been half so entrancing. The modern Greeks, Australian bushmen, and natives of the East Indies, like myself, only see the ugly side of the superphysical, for the spirits that haunt their vegetation are irredeemably ugly, horribly terrifying, and fiendishly vindictive.

The idea that the dead often passed into trees is well illustrated in the classics. For example, Æneas, in his wanderings, strikes a tree, and is half-frightened out of his wits by a great spurt of blood. A hollow voice, typical of phantasms and apparently proceeding from somewhere within the trunk, then begs him to desist, going on to explain that the tree is not an ordinary tree but the metamorphosed soul of an unlucky wight called Polydorus, (he must have been unlucky, if only to have had such a name). Needless to say, Æneas, who was strictly a gentleman in spite of his aristocratic pretensions, at once dropped his axe and showed his sympathy for the poor tree-bound spirit in an abundant flow of tears, which must have satisfied, even, Polydorus. There is a very similar story in Swedish folk-lore. A voice in a tree addressed a man, who was about to cut it down, with these words, 'Friend, hew me not !' But the man on this occasion was not a gentleman, and, instead of complying with the modest request, only plied his axe the more heartily. To his horror – a just punishment for his barbarity – there was a most frightful groan of agony, and out from the hole he had made in the trunk, rushed a fountain of blood, real human blood. What happened then I cannot say, but I imagine that the woodcutter, stricken with remorse, whipped up his bandana from the ground, and did all that lay in his power – though he had not had the advantages of lessons in first aid – to stop the bleeding. One cannot help being amused at these marvellous stories, but, after all, they are not very much more wonderful than many of one's own ghostly experiences. At any rate, they serve to illustrate how widespread and venerable is the belief that trees – trees, perhaps, in particular – are closely associated with the occult.

Pixies ! What are pixies ? That they are not the dear, delightful, quaint little people Shakespeare so inimitably portrays in the *Midsummer Night's Dream*, is, I fear, only too readily acknowledged. I am told that they may be seen even now, and I know those who say that they have seen them, but that they are the mere shadows of those dainty creatures that used to gambol in the moonshine and help the poor and weary in their household work. The present-day pixies, whom I am loath to imagine are the descendants of the old-world pixies – though, of course, on the other hand, they may be merely degenerates, a much more pleasant alternative – are I think still to be occasionally encountered in lonely, isolated districts; such, for instance, as the mountains in the West of Ireland, the Hebrides, and other more or less desolate islands, and on one or two of the Cornish hills and moors.

Like most phantasms, the modern pixies are silent and elusive. They appear and disappear with equal abruptness, contenting themselves with merely gliding along noiselessly

95

from rock to rock, or from bush to bush. Dainty they are not, pretty they are not, and in stature only do they resemble the pixie of fairy tales; otherwise they are true vagrarians, grotesque and often harrowing.

In my *Ghostly Phenomena* I have given one or two accounts of their appearance in the West of England, but the nearest approach to pixies that I have myself seen, were phantasms that appeared to me, in 1903, on the Wicklow Hills, near Bray. I was out for a walk on the afternoon of Thursday, 18 May; the weather was oppressive, and the grey, lowering sky threatened rain, a fact which accounted for the paucity of pedestrians. Leaving my temporary headquarters, at Bray, at half-past one, I arrived at a pretty village close to the foot of the hills and immediately began the ascent. Selecting a deviating path that wound its way up gradually, I, at length, reached the summit of the ridge.

On and on I strolled, careless of time and distance, until a sudden dryness in my throat reminded me it must be about the hour at which I generally took tea. I turned round and began to retrace my steps homeward. The place was absolutely deserted; not a sign of a human being or animal anywhere, and the deepest silence. I had come to the brink of a slight elevation when, to my astonishment, I saw in the tiny plateau beneath, three extraordinary shapes. Standing not more than two feet from the ground, they had the most perfectly proportioned bodies of human beings, but monstrous heads; their faces had a leadish blue hue, like that of corpses; their eyes were wide open and glassy. They glided along slowly and solemnly in Indian file, their grey, straggling hair and loose white clothes rustling in the breeze; and on arriving at a slight depression in the ground, they sank and sank, until they entirely disappeared from view. I then descended from my perch, and made a thorough examination of the spot where they had vanished. It was firm, hard, caked soil, without hole or cover, or anything in which they could possibly have hidden. I was somewhat shocked, as indeed I always am after an encounter with the superphysical, but not so much shocked as I should have been had the phantasms been bigger. I visited the same spot subsequently, but did not see another manifestation.

To revert to trees – fascinating, haunting trees. Much credulity was at one time attached to the tradition that the tree on which Jesus Christ was crucified was an aspen, and that, thenceforth, all aspens were afflicted with a peculiar shivering. Botanists, scientists, and matter-of-fact people of all sorts pooh-pooh this legend, as, indeed, many people nowadays pooh-pooh the very existence of Christ. But something – you may call it intuition – I prefer to call it my Guardian Spirit – bids me believe both; and I do believe as much in the tradition of the aspen as in the existence of Christ. Moreover, this intuition or influence – the work of my Guardian Spirit – whether dealing with things psychical, psychological, or physical has never yet failed me. If it warns me of the presence of a phantasm, I subsequently experience some kind or other of spiritual phenomenon; if it bids me beware of a person, I am invariably brought to discover later on that that person's intentions have been antagonistic to me; and if it causes me to deter from travelling by a certain route, or on a certain day, I always discover afterwards that it was a very fortunate thing for me that I abided by its warning. That is why I attach great importance to the voice of my Guardian Spirit; and that is why, when it tells me that, despite the many obvious discrepancies and absurdities in the Scriptures, despite the character of the Old Testament God – who repels rather than attracts me – despite all this, there was a Jesus Christ who actually was a great and benevolent Spirit, temporarily incarnate, and who really did suffer on the Cross in the manner described in subsequent MSS., – I believe it all implicitly. I back the still, small voice of my Guardian Spirit against all the arguments scepticism can produce.

Very good, then. I believe in the existence and spirituality of Jesus Christ because of the biddings of my Guardian Spirit, and, for the very same reason, I attach credence to the tradition of the quivering of the aspen. The sceptic accounts for the shaking of this tree by showing that it is due to a peculiar formation in the structure of the aspen's foliage. This may be so, but that peculiarity of structure was created immediately after Christ's crucifixion, and was created as a memento, for all time, of one of the most unpardonable murders on record.

There is something especially weird, too, in the ash; something that suggests to my mind that it is particularly susceptible to superphysical influences. I have often sat and listened to its groaning, and more than once, at twilight, perceived the filmy outline of some fantastic figure writhed around its slender trunk.

John Timbs, F.S.A., in his book of *Popular Errors*, published by Crosby, Lockwood & Co. in 1880, quotes from a letter, dated 7 July 1606, thus: 'It is stated that at Brampton, near Gainsborough, in Lincolnshire, "an ash tree shaketh in body and boughs thereof, sighing and groaning like a man troubled in his sleep, as if it felt some sensible torment. Many have climbed to the top of it, who heard the groans more easily than they could below. But one among the rest, being on the top thereof, spake to the tree; but presently came down much aghast, and lay grovelling on the earth, three hours speechless. In the end reviving, he said: 'Brampton, Brampton, thou art much bound to pray!'" The Earl of Lincoln caused one of the arms of the ash to be lopped off and a hole bored through the body, and then was the sound, or hollow voice, heard more audibly than before, but in a kind of speech which they could not comprehend. This is the second wonderful ash produced by past ages in this district – according to tradition, Ethelreda's budding staff having shot out into the first.' So says the letter, and from my own experience of the ash, I am quite ready to accredit it with special psychic properties, though I cannot state I have ever heard it speak.

I believe it attracts phantasms in just the same way as do certain people, myself included, and certain kinds of furniture. Its groanings at night have constantly attracted, startled, and terrified me; they have been quite different to the sounds I have heard it make in the daytime; and often I could have sworn that, when I listened to its groanings, I was listening to the groanings of some dying person, and, what is more harrowing still, to some person I knew.

I have heard it said, too, that the most ghastly screams and gurgles have been heard proceeding from the ash tree planted in or near the site of murders or suicides, and as I sit here writing, a scene opens before me, and I can see a plain with one solitary tree – an ash – standing by a pool of water, on the margin of which are three clusters of reeds. Dark clouds scud across the sky, and the moon only shows itself at intervals. It is an intensely wild and lonely spot, and the cold, dank air blowing across the barren wastes renders it all the more inhospitable. No one, no living thing, no object is visible save the ash. Suddenly it moves its livid trunk,

sways violently, unnaturally, backwards and forwards –
once, twice, thrice; and there comes from it a cry, a most
piercing, agonising cry, half human, half animal, that dies
away in a wail and imparts to the atmosphere a sensation
of ice. I can hear the cry as I sit here writing; my memory
rehearses it; it was one of the most frightful, blood-curdling,
hellish sounds I ever endured; and the scene was on the
Wicklow hills in Ireland.

The narcotic plant, the mandrake, is also credited with
groaning, though I cannot say I have ever heard it. Though
there is nothing particularly psychic about the witch-hazel,
in the hands of certain people who are mediumistic, it will
indicate the exact spot where water lies under the ground.
The people who possess this faculty of discovering the
locality of water by means of the hazel, are named dowsers,
and my only wonder is that their undeniably useful faculty
is not more cultivated and developed.

To my mind, there is no limit to the possibilities suggested
by this faculty; for surely, if one species of tree possesses
attraction for a certain object in nature, there can be no
reason why other species of trees should not possess a similar
attraction for other objects in nature. And if they possess
this attraction for the physical, why not for the superphysical – why, indeed, should not 'ghosts' come within the
radius of their magnetism?

The palm and sycamore trees have invariably been associated with the spiritual, and made use of symbolically, as
the tree of life. An illustration, on a stele in the Berlin
Museum, depicts a palm tree from the stem of which pro-
ceeds two arms, one administering to a figure, kneeling
below, the fruit or bread of life; the other, pouring from a
vase the water of life.

On another, a later Egyptian stele, the tree of life is the
sycamore. There is no doubt that the Egyptians and
Assyrians regarded these two trees as susceptible only to
good psychic influences, they figure so frequently in illus-
trations of the benevolent deities. Nor were the Jews and
Christians behind in their recognition of the extraordinary
properties of these two trees, especially the palm. We find it
symbolically introduced in the decoration of Solomon's
Temple – on the walls, furniture, and vessels; whilst in
Christian mosaics it figures as the tree of life in Paradise
(*vide* Rev. xxii. 1, 2, and in the apsis of S. Giovanni

Laterans). It is even regarded as synonymous with Jesus Christ, as may be seen in the illuminated frontispiece to an *Evangelium* in the library of the British Museum, where the symbols of the four Evangelists, placed over corresponding columns of lessons from their gospels, are portrayed looking up to a palm tree, rising from the earth, on the summit of which is a cross, with the symbolical letters alpha and omega suspended from its arms.

I am, of course, only speaking from my own experience, but this much I can vouch for, that I have never heard of a palm tree being haunted by an evil spirit, whereas I have heard of several cases in which palm leaves or crosses cut from palms have been used, and apparently with effect, as preventives of injuries caused by malevolent occult demonstrations; and were I forced to spend a night in some lonely forest, I think I should prefer, viewing the situation entirely from the standpoint of psychical possibilities, that that forest should be composed partly or wholly of palms.

Before concluding this chapter, I must make a brief allusion to another type of spirit – the *Barrowvian* – that resembles the vagrarian and pixie, inasmuch as it delights in lonely places. Whenever I see a barrow, tumulus or druidical, circle, I scent the probability of phantasms – phantasms of a peculiar sort. Most ancient burial-places are haunted, and haunted by two species of the same genus : the one, the spirits of whatever prehistoric forms of animal life lie buried there; and the other, grotesque phantasms, often very similar to vagrarians in appearance, but with distinct ghoulish propensities and an inveterate hatred to living human beings. In my *Ghostly Phenomena* I have referred to the haunting of a druidical circle in the North of England, and also to the haunting of a house I once rented in Cornwall, near Castle on Dinas, by barrowvians; I have heard, too, of many cases of a like nature. I have, of course, often watched all night, near barrows or cromlechs, without any manifestations taking place; sometimes, even, without feeling the presence of the Unknown, though these occasions have been rare. At about two o'clock one morning, when I was keeping my vigil beside a barrow in the South of England, I saw a phenomenon in the shape of a hand – only a hand, a big, misty, luminous blue hand, with long crooked fingers. I could, of course, only speculate as to the owner of the hand, and I must confess that I postponed that speculation till I was safe and sound, and bathed in sunshine, within the doors of my own domicile.

Hauntings of this type generally occur where excavations have been made, a barrow broken into, or a dolmen removed; the manifestations generally taking the form of phantasms of the dead, the prehistoric dead. But phenomena that are seen there are, more often than not, things that bear little or no resemblance to human beings; abnormally tall, thin things with small, bizarre heads, round, rectangular, or cone-shaped, sometimes semi or wholly animal, and always expressive of the utmost malignity. Occasionally, in fact I might say often, the phenomena are entirely bestial – such, for example, as huge, blue, or spotted dogs, shaggy bears, and monstrous horses. Houses, built on or near the site of such burial-places, are not infrequently disturbed by strange noises, and the manifestations, when materialized, usually take one or other of these forms. In cases of this kind I have found that exorcism has little or no effect; or, if any, it is that the phenomena become even more emphatic.

VAMPIRES, WERE-WOLVES, FOX-WOMEN, ETC.

Elliott O'Donnell

Vampires

According to a work by Jos Ennemoses, entitled *The Phantom World*, Hungary was at one time full of vampires. Between the river Theiss and Transylvania, were (and still are, I believe) a people called Heyducs, who were much pestered with this particularly noxious kind of phantasm. About 1732, a Heyduc called Arnauld Paul was crushed to death by a waggon. Thirty days after his burial a great number of people began to die, and it was then remembered that Paul had said he was tormented by a vampire. A consultation was held and it was decided to exhume him. On digging up his body, it was found to be red all over and literally bursting with blood, some of which had forced a passage out and wetted his winding sheet. Moreover, his hair, nails, and beard had grown considerably. These being sure signs that the corpse was possessed by a vampire, the local bailie was fetched and the usual proceedings for the expulsion of the undesirable phantasm began. A stake, sharply pointed at one end, was handed to the bailie, who, raising it above his head, drove it with all his might into the heart of the corpse. There then issued from the body the most fearful screams, whereupon it was at once thrown into a fire that had been specially prepared for it, and burned to ashes. But, though this was the end of that particular vampire, it was by no means the end of the hauntings; for the deaths, far from decreasing in number, continued in rapid succession, and no less than seventeen people in the village died within a period of three months. The question now arose as to which of the other bodies in the cemetery were 'possessed,' it being very evident that more than one vampire lay buried there. Whilst the matter was at the height of discussion, the solution to the problem was brought about thus. A girl, of the name of Stanoska, awoke in the middle of the night, uttering the most heart-rending screams, and declaring that the son of a man called Millo (who had been dead nine weeks) had nearly strangled her. A rush was at once made to the cemetery, and a general disinterment taking place, seventeen out of the forty corpses (including that of the son of Millo) showed unmistakable signs of vampirism. They were all treated according to the mode described, and their ashes cast into the adjacent river. A committee of inquiry concluded that the spread of vampirism had been due to the eating of certain cattle, of which Paul had been the first to partake. The disturbances ceased with the death of the girl and the destruction of her body, and the full account of the hauntings, attested to by officers of the local garrison, the chief surgeons, and the most influential of the inhabitants of the district, was sent to the Imperial Council of War at Venice, which caused a strict inquiry to be made into the matter, and were subsequently, according to Ennemoses, satisfied that all was *bona fide*.

In another work, *A History of Magic*, Ennemoses also refers to a case in the village of Kisilova, in Hungary, where the body of an old man, three days after his death, appeared to his son on two consecutive nights, demanding something to eat, and, being given some meat, ate it ravenously. The third night the son died, and the succeeding day witnessed the deaths of some five or six others. The matter was reported to the Tribunal of Belgrade, which promptly sent two officers to inquire into the case. On their arrival the old man's grave was opened, and his body found to be full of blood and natural respiration. A stake was then driven through its heart, and the hauntings ceased.

Though far fewer in number than they were, and more than ever confined to certain localities, I am quite sure that vampires are by no means extinct. Their modes and habits – they are no longer gregarious – have changed with the modes and habits of their victims, but they are none the less vampires. Have I seen them? No! but my not having been thus fortunate, or rather unfortunate, does not make me so discourteous as to disbelieve those who tell me that they have seen a vampire – that peculiar, indefinably peculiar shape that, wriggling along the ground from one tombstone to another, crawls up and over the churchyard wall, and making for the nearest house, disappears through one of its upper windows. Indeed, I have no doubt that had I watched that house some few days afterwards, I should have seen a pale, anæmic looking creature, with projecting teeth and a thoroughly imbecile expression, come out of it. I believe a large percentage of idiots and imbecile epileptics owe their pitiable plight to vampires which, in their infancy, they had the misfortune to attract. I do not think that, as of old, the vampires come to their prey installed in stolen bodies, but that they visit people wholly in spirit form, and, with their superphysical mouths, suck the brain cells dry of intellect. The baby, who is thus the victim of a vampire, grows up into something on a far lower scale of intelligence than dumb animals, more bestial than monkeys, and more dangerous (far more dangerous, if the public only realized it) than tigers; for, whereas the tiger is content with one square meal a day, the hunger of vampirism is never satisfied, and the half-starved, mal-shaped brain cells, the prey of vampirism, are in a constant state of suction, ever trying to draw in mental sustenance from the healthy brain cells around them. Idiots and epileptics are the cephalopoda of the land – only, if anything, fouler, more voracious, and more insatiable than their aquatic prototypes. They never ought to be at large. If not destroyed in their early infancy (which one cannot help thinking would be the most merciful plan both for the idiot and the community in general), those polyp brains ought to be kept in some isolated place where they would have only each other to feed upon. When I see an idiot walking in the streets, I always take very good care to give him a wide berth, as I have no desire that the vampire buried in his withered brain cells should derive any nutrition at my expense. From the fact that some towns which are close to cromlechs, ancient burial-grounds, woods, or moors are full of idiots, leads me to suppose that vampires often frequent the same spots as barrowvians, vagrarians and other types of elementals. Whilst, on the other hand, since many densely crowded centres have fully their share of idiots, I am led to believe that vampires are equally attracted by populous districts, and that, in short, unlike barrowvians and vagrarians, they can be met with pretty nearly everywhere. And now for examples.

A man I know, who spends most of his time in Germany, once had a strange experience when staying in the neighbourhood of the Hartz mountains. One sultry evening in August he was walking in the country, and noticed a perambulator with a white figure, which he took to be that of a remarkably tall nursemaid, bending over it. As he drew nearer, however, he found that he had been mistaken. The figure was nothing human; it had no limbs; it was cylindrical. A faint, sickly sound of sucking caused my friend to start forward with an exclamation of horror, and as he did so, the phantasm glided away from the perambulator and disappeared among the trees. The baby, my friend assured me, was a mere bag of bones, with a ghastly, grinning anæmic face. Again, when touring in Hungary, he had a similar experience. He was walking down a back street in a large, thickly populated town, when he beheld a baby lying on the hot and sticky pavement with a queer-looking object stooping over it. Wondering what on earth the thing was, he advanced rapidly, and saw, to his unmitigated horror, that it was a phantasm with a limbless, cylindrical body, a huge flat, pulpy head, and protruding, luminous lips, which were tightly glued to the infant's ears; and again my friend heard a faint, sickly sound of sucking, and a sound more hideously nauseating, he informed me, could not be imagined. He was too dumbfounded to act; he could only stare; and the phantasm, after continuing its loathsome occupation for some seconds, leisurely arose, and moving away with a gliding motion, vanished in the yard of an adjacent house. The child did not appear to be human, but a concoction of half a dozen diminutive bestialities, and as my friend gazed at it, too fascinated for the moment to tear himself away, it smiled up at him with the hungry, leering smile of vampirism and idiocy.

So much for vampires in the country and in crowded cities, but, as I have already remarked, they are ubiquitous. As an illustration, there is said to be a maritime town in a remote part of England, which, besides being full of quaintness (of a kind not invariably pleasant) and of foul smells, is also full of more than half-savage fishermen and idiots; idiots that often come out at dusk, and greatly alarm strangers by running after them.

Some years ago, one of these idiots went into a stranger's house, took a noisy baby out of its cot, and after tubbing it well (which I think showed that the idiot possessed certain powers of observation), cut off its head, throwing the offending member into the fire. The parents were naturally indignant, and so were some of the inhabitants; but the affair was speedily forgotten, and although the murderer was confined to a lunatic asylum, nothing was done to rid the town of other idiots who were, collectively, doing mischief of a nature far more serious than that of the recently perpetrated murder.

The wild and rugged coast upon which the town is situated was formerly the hunting-ground of wreckers, and I fear the present breed of fishermen, in spite of their hypocritical pretentions to religion, prove only too plainly by their abominable cruelty to birds and inhospitable treatment of strangers, that they are in reality no better than their forbears. This inherited strain of cruelty in the fishermen would alone account for the presence of vampires and every other kind of vicious elemental; but the town has still another attraction – namely, a prehistoric burial-ground, on a wide expanse of thinly populated moorland – in its rear.

A propos of vampires, my friend Mrs. South writes to me as follows (I quote her letter *ad verbum*) : 'The other night, I was dining with a very old friend of mine whom I had not seen for years, and, during a pause in the conversation, he suddenly said, "Do you believe in vampires?" I wondered for a moment if he had gone mad, and I think, in my matter-of-fact way, I blurted out something of the sort; but I saw in a moment, from the expression in his eyes, that he had something to tell me, and that he was not at all in the mood to be laughed at or misunderstood. "Tell me," I said, "I am listening." "Well," he replied, "I had an extraordinary experience a few months ago, and not a word of it have I breathed to any living soul. But sometimes the horror of it so overpowers me that I feel I must share my secret with someone; and you – well, you and I have always been such pals." I answered nothing, but gently pressed his hand.

'After lighting a cigarette, he commenced his story, which I will give you as nearly as possible in his own words :—

' "It is about six months ago since I returned from my travels. Up to that time I had been away from England for nearly three years, as you know. About a couple of nights after my return, I was dining at my Club, when someone tapped me on the shoulder, and turning round, I saw my old friend S——.

' "As I had no idea he was in London, you may imagine my delight. He joined me at dinner and we went over old times together. He asked me if I had heard anything of our mutual friend G——, to whom we were both very much attached. I said I had had a few lines from him about six months previously, announcing his marriage, but that I had never heard from him nor seen him since. He had settled, I believe, in the heart of the country. S—— then told me that he had not seen G—— since his engagement, neither had he heard from him; in fact he had written to him once or twice, but his letters had received no answer. There were whispered rumours that he was looking ill and unhappy. Hearing this, I got G——'s address from S——, and made up my mind I would run down and see him as soon as I could get away from town.

'"About a week afterwards I found myself, after driving an interminable distance, so it seemed to me, through Devonshire lanes, stopping outside a beautiful house which appeared to be entirely isolated from any other dwelling.

'"A few more minutes and I was standing before a blazing log fire in a fine old hall, eagerly awaiting the welcome I knew my old friend would give me. I did not anticipate long; in less time than it takes to tell G—— appeared, and with slow, painfully slow steps, crossed the hall to greet me. He was wasted to a shadow, and I felt a lump rise in my throat as I thought of the splendid, athletic boy I used to know. He made no excuse for his wife, who did not accompany him; and though I was naturally anxious to see her, I was glad that Jack and I were alone. We chatted together utterly regardless of the time, and it was not until the first gong had sounded that I thought of dressing for dinner. After performing a somewhat hurried toilette, I was hastening downstairs, when I suddenly became conscious that I was being watched. I looked all round and could see no one. I then heard a low, musical laugh just above my head, and looking up, I saw a figure leaning over the banisters. The beauty of the face dazzled me for a moment, and the loveliness of the eyes, which looked into mine and seemed to shine a red gold, held me spellbound. Presently a voice, every whit as lovely as the face, said : 'So you are Jack's chum?' The most beautiful woman I have ever seen then came slowly down the stairs, and slipping her arm through mine, led me to the dining-room. As her hand rested on my coat-sleeve, I remember noticing that the fingers were long, and thin, and pointed, and the nails so polished that they almost shone red. Indeed, I could not help feeling somewhat puzzled by the fact that everything about her shone red with the exception of her skin, which, with an equal brilliancy, shone white. At dinner she was lively, but she ate and drank very sparingly, and as though food was loathsome to her.

' "Soon after dinner I felt so exceedingly tired and sleepy, a most unusual thing for me, that I found it absolutely impossible to keep awake, and consequently asked my host and hostess to excuse me. I woke next morning feeling languid and giddy, and, while shaving, I noticed a curious red mark at the base of my neck. I imagined I must have cut myself shaving hurriedly the evening before, and thought nothing more about it.

' "The following night, after dinner, I experienced the same sensation of sleepiness, and felt almost as if I had been drugged. It was impossible for me to keep awake, so I again asked to be excused! On this occasion, after I had retired, a curious thing happened. I dreamed – or at least I suppose I dreamed – that I saw my door slowly open, and the figure of a woman carrying a candle in one hand, and with the other carefully shading the flame, glide noiselessly into my room. She was clad in a loose red gown, and a great rope of hair hung over one shoulder. Again those red-gold eyes looked into mine; again I heard that low musical laugh; and this time I felt powerless either to speak or to move. She leaned down, nearer and nearer to me; her eyes gradually assumed a fiendish and terrible expression; and with a sucking noise, which was horrible to hear, she fastened her crimson lips to the little wound in my neck. I remembered nothing more until the morning. The place on my neck, I thought, looked more inflamed, and as I looked at it, my dream came vividly back to me and I began to wonder if after all it was only a dream. I felt frightfully rotten, so rotten that I decided to return to town that day; and yet I yielded to some strange fascination, and determined, after all, to stay another night. At dinner I drank sparingly; and, making the same excuse as on the previous nights, I retired to bed at an early hour. I lay awake until midnight, waiting for I know not what; and was just thinking what a mad fool I was, when suddenly the door gently opened and again I saw Jack's wife. Slowly she came towards me, gliding as stealthily and noiselessly as a snake. I waited until she leaned over me, until I felt her breath on my cheek, and then – then flung my arms round her. I had just time to see the mad terror in her eyes as she realized I was awake, and the next instant, like an eel, she had slipped from my grasp, and was gone. I never saw her again. I left early the next morning, and I shall never forget dear old Jack's face when I said good-bye to him. It is only a few days since I heard of his death." '

Were-wolves

Closely allied to the vampire is the were-wolf, which, how-ever, instead of devouring the intellect of human beings, feeds only on their flesh. Like the vampire, the were-wolf belongs to the order of elementals; but, unlike the vampire, it is confined to a very limited sphere – the wilds of Norway, Sweden, and Russia, and only appears in two guises, that of a human being in the daytime and a wolf at night. I have closely questioned many people who have travelled in those regions, but very few of them – one or two at the most – have actually come in contact with those to whom the existence of the were-wolf is not a fable but a fact. One of these travellers, a mere acquaintance whom I met in an hotel in the Latin Quarter of Paris, assured me that the authenticity of a story he would tell me, relating to the were-wolf, was, in the neighbourhood through which he travelled, never for a single moment doubted.

My informant, a highly cultured Russian, spoke English, French, German, and Italian with as great fluency as I spoke my native tongue, and I believed him to be perfectly genuine. The incident he told me, to which unanimous belief was accredited, happened to two young men (whom I will call Hans and Carl), who were travelling to Nijni Novgorod, a city in the province of Tobolsk. The route they took was off the beaten track, and led them through a singularly wild and desolate tract of country. One evening, when they were trotting mechanically along, their horses suddenly came to a standstill and appeared to be very much frightened. They inquired of the driver the reason of such strange behaviour, and he pointed with his whip to a spot on the ice – they were then crossing a frozen lake – a few feet ahead of them. They got out of the sleigh, and, approaching the spot in-dicated, found the body of a peasant lying on his back, his throat gnawed away and all his entrails gone. 'A wolf with-out a doubt,' they said, and getting back into the sleigh, they drove on, taking good care to see that their rifles were ready for instant action. They had barely gone a mile when the horses again halted, and a second corpse was discovered, the corpse of a child with its face and thighs entirely eaten away. Again they drove on, and had progressed a few more miles when the horses stopped so abruptly that the driver was pitched bodily out; and before Carl and Hans could dismount, the brutes started off at a wild gallop. They were eventually got under control, but it was with the greatest difficulty that they were forced to turn round and go back, in order to pick up the unfortunate driver. The farther they went, the more restless they became, and when, at length, they approached the place where the driver had been thrown, they came to a sudden and resolute standstill. As no amount of whipping would now make them go on, Hans got out, and advancing a few steps, espied something lying across the track some little distance ahead of them. Gun in hand, he advanced a few more steps, when he suddenly stopped. To his utter amazement he saw, bending over a body, which he at once identified as that of their driver, the figure of a woman. She started as he approached, and, hastily springing up, turned towards him. The strange beauty of her face, her long, lithe limbs (she stood fully six feet high) and slender body, – the beauty of the latter enhanced by the white woollen costume in which she was clad, – had an extraordinary effect upon Hans. Her shining masses of golden hair, that curled in thick clusters over her forehead and about her ears; the perfect regularity of her features, and the lustrous blue of her eyes, enraptured him; whilst the expression both in her face and figure – in her sparkling eyes and firmly modelled mouth; in her red lips, and even in her pearly teeth, repulsed and almost frightened him. He gazed steadily at her, and, as he did so, the hold on his rifle involuntarily tightened. He then glanced from her face to her hands, and noticed with a spasm of horror that the tips of her long and beautifully shaped nails were dripping with blood, and that there was blood, too, on her knees and feet, blood all over her. He then looked at the driver and saw the wretched man's clothes had been partially stripped off, and that there were great gory holes in his throat and abdomen.

'Oh, I am so glad you have come!' the woman cried, addressing him in a strangely peculiar voice, that thrilled him to the marrow of his bones. 'It is the wolves. Do come and see what they have done. I saw them, from a distance, attack this poor man, and leaving my sleigh, for my horses came to a dead halt, and nothing I could do would induce them to move, I ran to his assistance. But, alas! I was too late!' Then, looking at her dress, from which Hans could scarcely remove his eyes, she cried out : 'Ugh! How disgusting – blood! My hands and clothes are covered with it. I tried to stop the bleeding, but it was no use'; and she proceeded to wipe her fingers on the snow.

'But why did you venture here alone?' Hans inquired, 'and why unarmed? How foolhardy! The wolves would have made short work of you had you encountered them!'

'Then you cannot have heard the report of my gun!' the woman cried, in well-feigned astonishment. 'How strange! I fired at the wolves from over there'; and she pointed with one of her slender, milky-white fingers to a spot on the ice some fifty yards away. 'Fortunately, they all made off,' she continued, 'and I hastened hither, dropping my gun that I might run the faster.'

'I can see no gun,' Hans exclaimed, shading his eyes with his hand and staring hard.

The woman laughed. 'What a disbelieving Jew it is!' she said. 'The gun is there; I can see it plainly. You must be short-sighted.' And then, straining her eyes on the far distance, she shrieked : 'Great Heavens! My sleigh has gone! Oh! what shall I do? What shall I do?'

Giving way to every gesture of despair, she looked so forlorn and beautiful that Hans would have been full of pity for her, had not certain vague suspicions, which he could neither account for nor overcome, entered his heart. Sorely perplexed, he did not know what to do, and stood looking at her in critical silence.

'Won't you come with me?' she said, clasping her hands beseechingly. 'Come with me to look for it. The horses may only have strayed a short distance, and we might overtake them without much difficulty.'

As she spoke thus, her piercing, earnest gaze thrilled him to the very soul, and his heart rose in rebellion against his reason. He had seen many fair women, but assuredly none as fair as this one. What eyes! What hair! What a complexion! What limbs! It seemed to him that she was not like ordinary women, that she was not of the same flesh and blood as any of the women he had ever met, and that she was in reality something far superior; something generated by the primitive glamour of the starry night, of the great, sparkling, ice-covered lake, and the lone, snow-capped peaks beyond. And all the while he was thinking thus, and unconsciously coming under the spell of her weird beauty, the woman continued to gaze entreatingly at him from under the long lashes which swept her cheeks. At last he could refuse her no longer – he would have gone to hell with her had she asked it – and shouting to Carl to remain where he was, he bade her lead the way. Setting off with long, quick strides that made Hans wonder anew, she soon put a considerable distance between herself and companion, and Carl. Hans now perceived a change; the sky grew dark, the clouds heavy, and the farther they went, the more perceptible this change became. The brightness and sense of joy in the air vanished, and, with its dissipation, came a chill and melancholy wind that rose from the bosom of the lake and swept all around them, moaning and sighing like a legion of lost souls.

But Hans, who came of a military stock, feared little, and, with his beautiful guide beside him, would cheerfully have faced a thousand devils. He had no eyes for anything save her, no thought of anything but her, and when she sidled up to him, playfully fingering his gun, he allowed her to take it from him and do what she liked with it. Indeed, he was so absorbed in the contemplation of her marvellous beauty, that he did not perceive her deftly unload his rifle and throw it from her on the ice; nor did he take any other notice than to think it a very pretty, playful trick when she laughingly caught his two hands, and bound them securely together behind his back. He was still drinking in the wondrous beauty of her eyes, when she suddenly slipped one of her pretty, shapely feet between his, and with a quick, subtle movement, tripped him and threw him to the ground. There was a dull crash, and, amid the hundred and one sounds that echoed and re-echoed through his head as it came in contact with the ice, he seemed to hear the far-off patter of horses' hoofs. Then something deliciously soft and cool touched his throat, and opening his eyes, he found his beautiful companion bending over him and undoing the folds of his woollen neckerchief with her shapely fingers. For such an experience he would fall and faint till further orders. He sought her eyes, and all but fainted again – the expression in them appalled him. They were no longer those of a woman but a devil, a horrible, sordid devil that hungered not merely for his soul, but for his flesh and blood. Then, in a second, he understood it all – she was a were-wolf, one of those ghastly creatures he had hitherto scoffingly attributed to the idle superstitions of the peasants. It was she who had mutilated the bodies they had passed on the road; it was she who had killed and half-eaten their driver; it was she – but he could think no more, it was all too horrible, and the revulsion of his feelings towards her clogged his brain. He longed to grapple with her, strangle her, and he could do nothing. The bare touch of those fingers – those cool, white, tapering fingers, with their long, shining filbert nails, all ready and eager to tear and rend his flesh to pieces – had taken all the life from his limbs, and he could only gaze feebly at her and damn her from the very bottom of his soul. One by one, more swiftly now, she unfastened the buttons of his coat and vest and then, baring her cruel teeth with a soft gurgle of excitement, and a smack of her red glistening lips, she prepared to eat him. Strangely enough, he experienced no pain as her nails sank into the flesh of his throat and chest and clawed it asunder. He was numb, numb with the numbness produced by hypnotism or paralysis – only some of his faculties were awake, vividly, startlingly awake. He was abruptly roused from this state by the dull crack of a rifle, and an agonizing, blood-curdling scream, after which he knew no more till he found himself sitting upright on the ice, gulping down brandy, his throat a mass of bandages, and Carl kneeling beside him.

'Where is she?' he asked, and Carl pointed to on object on the ice. It was the body of a huge white wolf, with half its head blown away.

'An explosive bullet,' Carl said grimly. 'I thought I would make certain of the beast, even at the risk of hurting you; and, mein Gott! it was a near shave! You have lost some of your hair, but nothing more. When I saw you go away with the woman, I guessed something was up. I did not like the look of her at all; she was a giantess, taller than any woman I have ever seen; and the way she had you in tow made me decidedly uncomfortable. Consequently, I followed you at a distance, and when I saw her trip you, I lashed up our horses and came to your rescue as fast as I could. Unfortunately, I had to dismount when I was still some distance off, as no amount of lashing would induce the horses to approach you nearer, and after arriving within range, it took me some seconds to get my rifle ready and select the best position for a shot. But, thank God! I was just in time, and, beyond a few scratches, you are all right. Shall we leave the beast here or take it with us?'

'We will do neither,' Hans said, with a shudder, whilst a new and sad expression stole into his eyes. 'I cannot forget it was once a woman! and, my God! what a woman! We will bury her here in the ice.'

The story here terminated, and from the fact that I have heard other stories of a similar nature, I am led to believe that there is in this one some substratum of truth. Were-wolves are not, of course, always prepossessing; they vary considerably. Moreover, they are not restricted to one sex, but are just as likely to be met with in the guise of boys and men as of girls and women.

Fox-women

Very different from this were-wolf, though also belonging to the great family of elementals, are the fox-women of Japan and China, about which much has been written, but about which, apparently, very little is known.

In China the fox was (and in remote parts still is) believed to attain the age of eight hundred or a thousand years. At fifty it can assume the form of a woman, and at one hundred that of a young and lovely girl, called Kao-Sai, or 'Our Lady.' On reaching the thousand years' limit, it goes to Paradise without physical dissolution. I have questioned many Chinese concerning these fox-women, but have never been able to get any very definite information. One China-man, however, assured me that his brother had actually seen the transmigration from fox to woman take place. The man's name I have forgotten, but I will call him Ching Kang. Well, Ching Kang was one day threading his way through a lovely valley of the Tapa-ling mountains, when he came upon a silver (*i.e.* white) fox crouching on the bank of a stream in such a peculiar attitude that Ching Kang's attention was at once arrested. Thinking that the animal was ill, and delighted at the prospect of lending it aid, for silver foxes are regarded as of good omen in China, Ching Kang approached it, and was about to examine it carefully, when to his astonishment he found he could not move – he was hypnotised. But although his limbs were paralysed, his faculties were wonderfully active, and his heart almost ceased beating when he saw the fox slowly begin to get bigger and bigger, until at last its head was on a level with his own. There was then a loud crash, its skin burst asunder, and there stepped out of it the form of a girl of such entrancing beauty that Ching Kang thought he must be in Heaven. She was fairer than most Chinese women; her eyes were blue instead of brown, and her shapely hands and feet were of milky whiteness. She was gaily dressed in blue silk, with earrings and bracelets of blue stone, and carried in one of her hands a blue fan. With a wave of her slender palms she released Ching Kang from his spell, and, bidding him follow her, plunged into a thick clump of bushes. Madly infatuated, Ching Kang needed no second bidding, but, keeping close to her heels, stolidly pushed his way through barricades of brambles that, whilst yielding to her touch, closed on him and beat him on the face and body so unmercifully that in a very short time he was barely recognizable, being literally bathed in blood. However, despite his wounds increasing and multiplying with every step he took, and naturally causing him the most excruciating agony, Ching Kang never, for one instant, thought of turning back; he always kept within touching distance of the blue form in front of him. But at last human nature could stand it no longer; his strength gave way, and as with a mad shriek of despair he implored her to stop, his senses left him and he fell in a heap to the ground. When he recovered he was lying alone, quite alone in the middle of the road, exactly opposite the spot where he had first seen the fox, and by his side was a fan, a blue fan. Picking it up sadly, he placed it near his heart (where it remained to the very day of his death), and with one last lingering look at the bank of the stream, he continued his solitary journey.

This was Ching Kang's story. His brother did not think he ever met the fox-woman again. He believed Ching Kang was still searching for her when he died.

MODERN WITCHCRAFT

Robert Graves

Witches have made headlines recently both in Germany and England. Mob violence is reported from Franconia, a Catholic province with a somewhat backward peasant population, against half-crazed old women accused of bewitching their neighbours. Farmer Sepp's best cow dies mysteriously, lice infest his house, his well dries up, his wife miscarries. Who is to blame? Old Mitzi, of course, who lives at the end of the land and once mumbled something nasty when Farmer Sepp accused her of stealing his apples. Nobody likes Old Mitzi, and the cat is doubtless a demonic familiar.

Julius Streicher, Nazi editor of *Der Sturmer* and Gauleiter of Franconia, exploited these old-fashioned witch-hunting instincts when he blamed the Jews for all Germany's ills. Now that the Jews have all gone, peasants vent their spite on witches again.

The sudden spread of organized witch groups in modern Britain follows naturally from Dr. Margaret Murray's anthropological studies, *Witchcraft in Western Europe* and *The God of the Witches*, published a generation ago. She surprised her readers by presenting witches as members of an ancient British fertility cult – akin to those of Greece, Italy and Germany – whom the Christians persecuted for their stubborn traditionalism and who, despite all witness to the contrary, were harmless enough.

Until then, the popular view of witches had been the semi-comic Victorian one of the old crones in steeple hats riding through the moonlit air on brooms. Witch-hunts were ascribed to mass-hysteria, like the frequent reports of flying saucers a few years ago; and lawyers could smile at our famous legal authority, Blackstone of *The Commentaries*, who wrote : 'To deny the possibility, nay, the actual existence of witchcraft, is to contradict the revealed world of God.'

Blackstone had in mind I Samuel xxviii, 7–25, when the Witch of Endor raised up Samuel's ghost for Saul. But he can have placed little reliance in the confessions of supposed witches, extorted under the Witchcraft Act of 1541 by inquisitors armed with the official handbook, *Malleus Maleficarum*, or *Hammer of Witches*. Witch trials had been a public scandal at the time, although Elizabeth's inquisitors did not use the rack, hot tongs, tooth-drawing, or other crude Continental methods which violated English Common Law. The witch's alleged crimes – of blasting crops, producing abortions in women and impotence in men, causing murrain among cattle, raising gales to wreck ships, killing by use of wax images or direct means – were all subsidiary to a greater sin of a pact with the Devil. Confession of this sin was readily obtained by anticipation of modern brain-washing techniques.

The word witch derives from the Anglo-Saxon *wicca*, 'a magician who weakens the power of evil'; and it was held that these 'powers of evil' could be identified and weakened only by a priest. A witch was taking too much on himself by his spells. Before the Norman Conquest, however, a proved witch had merely to do penance, though in some cases for as much as seven years; it was not until 1562 that he could be condemned to death. Many thousands of witches were then hanged : most charges being prompted by fear, malice, revenge, hope of gain, or sheer fanaticism – just as, in wartime, spies are seen everywhere.

King James I intervened personally at the trial of the North Berwick witches, who confessed that they had attempted to wreck his ship by throwing a christened cat into the sea. This offended his common sense, and he shouted out that they lied. But Agnes Sampson, a leader of the coven answered quietly that she did not wish him to think her a liar. Drawing James aside, she repeated word for word the conversation which had passed between him and his Danish queen in bed on their wedding night. Such manifest proof of second sight filled him with fear : and the witches were accordingly hanged.

Witch-hunting in England was largely the sport of Puritans. They took to heart the Mosaic command in Exodus xxii, 18 : 'Thou shalt not suffer a witch to live !' Though a distinction had been hitherto made between 'white witches', who did cures or told fortunes in the name of the Virgin or the Saints, and the 'black witches', who followed their own dark devices, a witch's colour made no odds to the Puritans. After the Reformation their madness slowly cooled, but it was not until George II's reign that the various Witchcraft Acts were replaced by one making the crime punishable only if used for monetary fraud.

In 1950, this was superseded by the 'Fraudulent Mediums Act', when a confession of witchcraft became no more dangerous than that of atheism. Three or four covens seem somehow to have survived in England when Dr. Murray's sympathetic reassessment of organized witchcraft made a revival possible. It was helped by Britain's rapid de-Christianization, which did not imply a moral decline, but rather a criticism of church-going as inadequate to spiritual needs and out-of-step with history and science. Some of the younger generation took to ideal Communism or Nuclear Disarmament. But the witch cult, presented by Dr. Murray as a more ancient form of worship than Christianity, attracted the daredevils.

Its revival allowed full play to the stronger human emotions. Witches met secretly in wooded country, not in cold Gothic cathedrals or red-brick chapels. Women took as important a part in the dancing, singing, and feasting as men. Each 'coven' consisted of six pairs, either husbands and wives, or engaged couples, and an officiating priestess. All went naked. Tests of fortitude under flagellation and horrific danger, the raising of spirits, cauldron stirrings, incense-burning, love feasts, round-dances performed back to back, served one main purpose : that of reaching an ecstatic state in which the magnetic force of the whole coven was focused on some unanimously chosen object. Strange phenomena were then experienced – among them, it was said, visions of past and future. To concentrate this force, the rites were formed in a magic circle cut on turf.

I am not a witch myself and have never assisted at any Sabbath. Although most English witches of my acquaintance are honest idealists, the craft attracts hysterical or perverted characters and, there being no longer a Grand Master or Chief Devil to discipline them, schisms and dissolutions are frequent in covens.

The main architect of this revival was an elderly Scottish anthropologist, now dead, Dr. Gerald Gardner, curator of a Witchcraft Museum in the Isle of Man, and author of *Witchcraft Today*, a popular apology for his fellow-witches. Dr. Gardner was first initiated into a Hertfordshire coven whose traditions had, it seems, been reinterpreted by a group of theosophists before being aligned with his own views of what young witches need in the way of fun and games. A female deity whom Dr. Gardner identified with the ancient European Moon-goddess, was preferred to Dr. Murray's Horned God.

Witchcraft Today, with a foreword by Dr. Murray, excited immediate attention. Sensational attacks made on Dr. Gardner by the British Press as 'a devil worshipper who puts around the dangerous idea that witchcraft is not evil' seems to have been based on Montague Summers' highly coloured accounts of diabolism and blood sacrifice in his *Witchcraft and Black Magic*. Dr. Gardner who believes in neither the devil nor in blood sacrifice received hundreds of fan-letters and applications for admittance to witch covens.

Apparently the equal division of the sexes in modern covens is Dr. Gardner's contribution to the craft; for Dr. Murray shows that although every medieval coven had its Maiden as assistant to the Chief, men were in the majority.

That witches existed in Britain from early times is undeniable. Members of a surviving Somersetshire coven still carry small blue tattoos in woad pricked below a particular finger joint, which stands for a letter in the pre-Christian Celtic alphabet. They call themselves 'Druids', worship a neolithic British god, and meet at cross-quarter-days – Candlemas, May Eve, Lammas, and Hallowe'en – in a Druidic stone circle. Nevertheless, I suspect that their traditions are based on reforms made by some late eighteenth-century antiquarian of the Edward Davies school.

Druids are chosen, after puberty, for certain natural powers of intuition and diagnosis, second sight, and thought control. Their membership, though tending to run in local families, includes professional men and women from London and Bristol. Their practices are very different from the spell-casting, love-philtres, poisonings and blackmail of ancient Franconian, or indeed present-day Majorcan, witches! There is a village carpenter, living not many miles from my home in Majorca, whose wife, hearing that he was in love with the baker's daughter, once put a spell on him. He could no longer cross the doorstep into the street without fainting; not for 13 years. Then his wife died, he followed her coffin across the threshold and is now happily married to the baker's daughter.

Dr. Murray, Miss Christina Hole, Mr. Mervyn Peake, the late Charles Williams, and other investigators seem to have ignored one important fact about the medieval witch cult: that it was brought to Europe by the Saracens, and grafted on a pagan Celtic stock. The Saracens had seized Spain in 711 A.D. (and were not expelled until 1492), controlled southern France by 889, and soon added to it Savoy, Piedmont, and part of Switzerland. Their witch groups, like the dervishes, were devoted to ecstatic dancing, miraculous cures, and the pursuit of wisdom personified as a Divine Woman, from whom comes The Queen of Elphame, beloved by Thomas the Rhymer and other Scottish witch-men.

The God of the witches is held by Dr. Murray to be a lineal descendant of a paleolithic Goat or Stag-god who later became the Gaulish Cernunnus, and Shakespeare's Herne the Hunter. Yet the lighted candle which every Grand Master, disguised as a black he-goat, wore between his horns on the great Witches' Sabbath – whether in England or in France – points in a very different direction. Idries Shah Sayed, the Sufi historian, has shown that a candle set between two horns emblemised the ninth-century Aniza school of mystics, founded by Abu-el-Ataahia. Abu came from the powerful Arabian Aniza (Goat) tribe, to which our contemporaries, Ibn Saud's sons and the Ruler of Kuwait both belong. The candle therefore meant 'illumination from the head of Aniza'.

'Robin', the generic name for a Chief or Grand Master, represents the Persian *Rah-bin* ('he who sees the road'). A Berber off-shoot of the Aniza school was known as 'the Two-Horned', and in Spain lived under the protection of the Aragonese Kings, who intermarried alike with the Prophet's royal descendants at Granada and with the English monarchy.

It is evidently this particular cult that reached the British Isles. An illustration on the cover of *Sadducismus Triumphantus*, a 1681 chap-book, shows Robin Goodfellow, horns on his head and candle in hand, capering among a coven of witches who number 13 like the Berber groups. A Two-Horned devotee wore his ritual knife, the *ad-dbamne* ('athame' to present-day witches) unsheathed and, as a reminder of his mortality, danced in a *kafan*, or winding-sheet (which is the most probable derivation of coven), at a meeting known as *az zabat*, 'the Powerful Occasion'. Hence the 'Witches Sabbath', or 'Esbar'. Two beautiful young French witches told De Lancre, an examiner at La Bourd, that their Sabbath was a paradise of inexpressible joy, a prelude to still greater glory, and far better than the Mass. The Two-Horned did indeed consider ecstasy no more than a prelude to divine wisdom. Some of them rode sticks, or brooms, like hobby-horses; cantering 'widder-shins', against the course of the sun, as around the Kaaba at Mecca; which explains why English witches were accused of causing storms, mildew, and blight by this means. Modern witches are careful to dance in the sun-wise direction.

It is not known at what period the Two-Horned cult entered Britain. The climate was favourable in 1208, when the Pope laid England under an Interdict for ten years, and King John sent an embassy to Morocco with secret promises that he would turn Moslem. And again, 100 years later, when the entire Order of Knights Templars was accused of witchcraft and suppressed at the Pope's orders.

The original school of Aniza achieved a state of ecstasy by beating drums and cymbals, or rhythmic clapping in ever-increasing tempo : but hallucigenetic drugs seem to have been preferred at a later period, lest the noise of Two-Horned revels might come to the ears of Church officers.

The earliest accounts of broomstick rides say nothing of levitation; later ones suggest that an English witch, when initiated, was blindfolded, smeared with toxic flying ointment, and set astride a broom. The ointment contained foxglove (digitalis) to accelerate the pulse, aconite to numb feet and hands, and belladonna, cowbane, or hemlock to confuse the senses. Other witches fanned the novice's face and, after a while, she could no longer feel her feet on the ground. The cry went up :

> *Horse and hattock,*
> *Horse and go,*
> *Horse and pellatis*
> *Ho, Ho!*

and she believed the Chief who told her she was flying across land and sea.

Loathing of the crucifix is attributed alike to Templars and witches, the crucifix being a graven image of the kind which Moses (supported by Jesus himself, and by Mahomed) forbade to be worshipped. Both witches and Templars were, in fact, Christians, though heretical ones. Robin Hood ballads, sung at May Games around a pagan Maypole, suggest that the Two-Horned cult had been active in the reign of Edward II, who enlisted Robin and his merry men as Royal archers. Robin and Maid Marian belonged to a coven of thirteen.

But the Two-Horned did not dance naked; nor did any medieval British witches. The modern cult has borrowed its nudism either from the Far East or from Germany – where souvenir shops in the Harz mountains have long been selling figurines of naked young Brocken *Hexen* astride brooms.

There is no need to worry about modern witches. In fact, they have a great many worries of their own : such as that of finding seclusion for their rites – difficult these days, except in private houses or at nudist camps. Also charges of obscenity and diabolism, still levelled at them by newspapers. The diabolic Black Masses described by Montague Summers are not witchcraft, but intellectual atheism : a revolt from within the Catholic Church against its prime mysteries.

In 1954, Dr. Gardner wrote gloomily about the future of witchcraft :

'I think we must say goodbye to the witch. The cult is doomed, I am afraid, partly because of modern conditions, housing shortage, the smallness of modern families, and chiefly by education. The modern child is not interested. He knows witches are all bunk.'

Yet the craft seems healthy enough now, and growing fast, though torn by schisms and Dr. Gardner's death. It now only needs some gifted mystic to come forward, reunite, and decently reclothe it, and restore its original hunger for wisdom. Fun and games are insufficient.

The very latest development is that certain reputable psychotherapists are considering the possibility of curing their more socially inhibited patients by a discipline based on modern witchcraft, after enlisting coven-leaders in their service. But psychological science, even if supported by a prolonged study of primitive magic, is insufficient. Like fun and games.

AN INDICTMENT FOR WITCHCRAFT

Anonymous

Annaple Thompsone, widow in Borrostowness and Margaret Pringle, wife of the deceased John Campbell, seivewright there, are indigtted and accused that whereas, notwithstanding the law of God particularlie set down in the Twentieth Chapter of Leveticus and the Eighteenth Chapter of Deuteronomy, and by the lawes and acts of Parliament of this kingdome and constant practis thereof, particularlie to the Twentyseventh act, 29 Parliament Q. Marie, the cryme of WITCHCRAFT is declaired to be one HORREID, ABOMINABLE AND CAPITAL CRYME, punishable with the pains of death and confiscation of moveables :— nevertheless it is of veritie, that you have committed and are gwyltie of the said cryme of WITCHCRAFT, in awa far ye have entered in practicion with the DEVILE, the enemie of your salvatoiwn, and have renownced our blessed Lord and Saviour, and your baptizme, and have given yoursellfes, both soulles and bodies, to the DEVILE, and wyth swyndrie witches, in divers places. And particularlie ye, the said Annaple Thompsone, had a metting with the DEVILE, in your coming betwixt Linlithgow and Borrostowness, where the DEVILE, in the lykeness of one black man, told you, that you was one poor puddled bodie, and had one lyiff and difficulties to win through the world; and promesed if you wald followe him, and go alongst with him, you should never want, but have one better lyiff; and about fyve weeks thereafter the DEVILE appeared to you, when you was going to the coal-hill, abowt seven a-clock in the morning. Having renewed his former temptatiown, you did condeshend thereto and declared yourself content to follow him and become his servant; and ye and other persones wis at several metting with the DEVILE, in the links of Borrostowness, and ye did eate and drink with the DEVILE, and with one another. And you, the said Margaret Pringle, have bein one witch this many yeeres bygone, hath renownced your baptizme and become the DEVILE'S servant, and promeis to follow him, and the DEVILE took you by the right hand, whereby it was for eight days greivowslie pained, but, having it twitched new again, it immedeatlie became haill. And ye both, and ilk of you, was at a metting with the DEVILE at the croce of Murestain, above Renneil, upon the threttein of October last, when you all danced, and the DEVILE acted the piper, and where you endevored to have destroyed Andrew Mitchell, sone to John Mitchell, elder in dean of Kenneil.

A PACT WITH THE DEVIL

Anonymous

Emperor Lucifer, master of all the rebellious spirits, I beseech thee be favourable to me in the calling which I make upon thy great DEMON MINISTER, having desire to make a pact with him; I pray thee also, Prince Beelzebub, to protect me in my undertaking. O Count Ashtoreth! be propitious to me, and cause that this night the great DEMON appear unto me in human form and without any evil smell, and that he grant me, by means of the pact which I shall deliver to him, all the riches of what I have need. O great DEMON, I beseech thee leave thy dwelling, in whatever part of the world it may be, to come and speak with me; if not, I will thereto compel thee by the power of the mighty words of the great Key of Solomon, whereof he made use to force the rebellious spirits to accept his pact. Appear, then, instantly, or I will continually torment thee by the mighty words of the Key: 'Aglon Tetagram Vaycheon Stimulamathon Erohares Retragsammathon Clyoran Icion Esition Existien Eryona Onera Erasyn Moyn Meffias Soter Emmanuel Sabaoth Adomai, I call you, Amen.'

The Devil will then appear and say:

I cannot grant thy demand but on condition that thou give me thyself at the end of seven years, so that I may do with thee, body and soul, what shall please me.

The Necromancer shall then throw the Devil his pact which must be written in his own hand on a small piece of virgin parchment and consisting of the following words signed with his own blood:

I promise great DEMON to repay him in seven years for all he shall give me.

In witness whereof I have signed ....

HOW TO RAISE A SPIRIT

Anonymous

It is decreed that if the ghost or apparition of a departed person is to be exorcised, the Magician, with his assistant, must repair to the churchyard or tomb where the deceased was buried, exactly at midnight, as the ceremony can only be performed in the night between the hours of twelve and one. The grave is first to be opened, or an aperture made by which access may be had to the naked body. The magician having described the circle, and holding a magic wand in his right hand, while his companion or assistant beareth a consecrated torch, he turns himself to all the four winds, and, touching the dead body three times with the magical wand, repeats as follows : By the virtue of the Holy Resurrection, and the torments of the damned, I conjure and exorcise thee, Spirit of N. deceased, to answer my liege demands, being obedient unto these sacred ceremonies, on pain of everlasting torment and distress . . . Berald, Beroald, Balbin, Gab, Gabor, Agaba. Arise, arise, I charge and command thee.

After these forms and ceremonies, the ghost or apparition will become visible, and will answer any questions put to it by the exorcist. But if it be desired to put interrogatories to the spirit of any corpse that has hanged, drowned, or otherwise made away with itself, the conjuration must be performed while the body lies on the spot where it is first found after the suicide hath been committed, and before it is touched or removed. The ceremony is as follows. The exorcist binds upon the top of his wand a bundle of St. John's wort or *Millies perforatum*, with the head of an owl; and having repaired to the spot where the corpse lies, at twelve o'clock at night, he draws the circle and solemnly repeats these words : By the mysteries of the deep, by the flames of Banal, by the power of the East and the silence of the night, by the Holy Rites of Hecate, I conjure and exorcise thee, thou distressed spirit, to present thyself here, and reveal unto me the cause of thy calamity, why thou didst offer violence to thy own liege life, where thou art now in being, and where thou wilt hereafter be.

Then gently smiting the carcase nine times with the rod, he adds : I conjure thee, thou Spirit of this N. deceased, to answer my demands that I propound unto thee, as thou ever hopest for the rest of the holy ones and ease of all thy misery; by the Blood of Jesus which He shed for thy soul, I conjure and bind thee to utter unto me what I shall ask thee.

Then, cutting down the carcase from the tree, they shall lay its head towards the east; in the space that this following conjuration is repeating, they shall set a chafing-dish of fire at its right hand, into which they shall pour a little wine, some mastic, and some gum-aromatic, and lastly [the contents of] a vial full of the sweetest oil. They shall have also a pair of bellows and some unkindled charcoal to make the fire burn bright when the carcase rises. The conjuration is this :

I conjure thee, thou Spirit of N., that thou do immediately enter into thy ancient body again, and answer to my demands, by the virtue of the Holy Resurrection, and by the posture of the body of the Saviour of the world, I charge thee, I conjure thee, I command thee, on pain of the torments and wandering of thrice seven years, which I, by the force of sacred magic rites, have power to inflict upon thee; by thy sighs and groans I conjure thee to utter thy voice. So help thee God and the prayers of the Holy Church. Amen.

This ceremony being thrice repeated, while the fire is burning with mastic and gum-aromatic, the body will begin to rise, and at last will stand upright before the exorcist, answering with a faint and hollow voice the questions propounded unto it : why it destroyed itself, where its dwelling is, what its food and life are, how long it will be ere it enter into rest, and by what means the magician may assist it to come to rest; also of the treasures of this world, where they are hid. Moreover, it can answer very punctually concerning the places where ghosts reside, and of the manner of communicating with them, teaching the nature of Astral Spirits and hellish beings so far as its capacity alloweth. All this when the ghost hath fully answered, the magician ought, out of commiseration and reverence to the deceased, to use what means can possibly be used for procuring rest unto the spirit, to which effect he must dig a grave, and, filling the same half full of quick-lime, with a little salt and common sulphur, must put the carcase naked into it. Next to the burning of the body into ashes, this is of great force to quiet and end the disturbance of the Astral Spirit. But in this and in all cases where the ghosts or apparitions of deceased persons are raised up and consulted, great caution is to be observed by the Magician to keep close within the circle; for if, by the constellation and position of the stars at his nativity, he be in the predicament of those who follow the Black Art for iniquitous purposes, it is very dangerous to conjure any spirits without describing the form of the circle, and wearing upon the heart, or holding in the hand, the Pentacle of Solomon. For the ghosts of men deceased can easily effect sudden death to the magician born under such a constellation of the planets, even whilst in the act of being exorcised.

THE BLACK GOAT OF BRANDENBURG

Anonymous

Another rare manuscript from the annals of necromancy –
fictional this time – is *The Black Goat of Brandenburg*. The
work of an unknown German author of the middle seventeenth century, the book details the activities of a group of
devil worshippers and their continuing search for still more
bestial methods to prove their devotion to evil. Each chapter
piles horror on horror and there can be little doubt that
the author was well versed in his subject. Unfortunately the
book has not survived the intervening years intact, but I
have been able to secure this fragment which I hope conveys
a little of the gruesome and bloody atmosphere of the work.

'Nothing,' exclaimed the sorcerer, 'but the immolation of
a perfect goat, without a single hair about him that is not
black, will propitiate my master, and secure the great object
for which we have so deeply laboured.'

The provinces of Russia, and the countries of Poland and
Lithuania were traversed in search of this precious animal,
which the devil worshippers at length obtained for the value
of its weight in gold.

The Black Goat was laid at the feet of their exorcist; who
now proceeded to accomplish his purpose of compelling
Lucifer to reveal the secret places, where all the treasures
were buried that in former times had disappeared from
Germany.

At midnight, on a heath near Berlin, and under the gibbet
of a newly hung murderer, these fanatics assembled, with
their conductor, to witness the consummation of this unholy
work. The struggling goat was slaughtered in the most barbarous manner, and single drops of its blood, wrung out in
the agonies of death, were sprinkled upon each of the followers.

The carcase then crackled in the flames of a red fire that
burnt before him, and hymns of impious adoration were
chanted to the deity of Hell.

These rites continued till dawn, when they were broken

in upon by a party of local officials; and though the infatuated assistants at this scene were permitted to escape, its
principal, the sorcerer, was dragged away to confinement,
and perished in the dungeons of Spandau.

THE CONFESSION OF THE WITCHES OF ELFDALE

Anonymous

In 1669 the people of the villages of Mohra and Elfdale in Sweden, believing that they were troubled by witches, were visited by a royal commission, the result of whose investigations was the execution of twenty-three adults and fifteen children; running of the gauntlet by thirty-six between the ages of nine and sixteen years; the lashing on the hand of twenty children for three Sundays at the church-door, and similar lashing of the aforesaid thirty-six once a week for a year. Portions of the confessions of the witches are given below from the Public Register.

We of the province of Elfdale do confess that we used to go to a gravel-pit which lay hard by a cross-way (Hecate), and there we put on a vest (Wolf-girdle) over our heads, and then danced round, and after this ran to the cross-way, and called the Devil thrice, first with a still voice, the second time somewhat louder, and the third time very loud, with these words – *Antecessor, come and carry us to Blockula.* Whereupon immediately he used to appear, but in different habits; but for the most part we saw him in a grey coat and red and blue stockings : he had a red beard (Barbarossa), a high-crowned hat (Turncap), with linen of divers colours wrapt about it, and long garters upon his stockings.

Then he asked us whether we would serve him with soul and body. If we were content to do so, he set us upon a beast which he had there ready, and carried us over churches and high walls; and after all we came to a green meadow where Blockula lies. We must procure some scrapings of altars, and filings of church clocks; and then he gives us a horn with a salve in it, wherewith we do anoint ourselves (chrism); and a saddle with a hammer (Thor's), and a wooden nail, thereby to fix the saddle (Walkyr's); whereupon we call upon the Devil and away we go.

For their journey, they said they made use of all sorts of instruments, of beasts, of men, of spits, and posts, according as they had opportunity : if they do ride upon goats (Azazel) and have many children with them, that all may have room, they stick a spit into the backside of the Goat, and then are anointed with the aforesaid ointment. What the manner of their journey is, God only knows. Thus much was made out, that if the children did at any time name the names (Egyptian spells) of those that had carried them away, they were again carried by force either to Blockula, or to the cross-way, and there miserably beaten, insomuch that some of them died of it.

A little girl of Elfdale confessed that, naming the name of JESUS as she was carried away, she fell suddenly upon the ground, and got a great hole in her side, which the Devil presently healed up again, and away he carried her; and to this day the girl confessed she had exceeding great pain in her side.

They unanimously confessed that Blockula is situated in a delicate large meadow, whereof you can see no end. The place or house they met at had before it a gate painted with divers colours; through this gate they went into a little meadow distinct from the other, where the beasts went that they used to ride on; but the men whom they made use of in their journey stood in the house by the gate in a slumbering posture, sleeping against the wall (castle of Waldemar). In a huge large room of this house, they said, there stood a very long table, at which the witches did sit down; and that hard by this room was another chamber where there were very lovely and delicate beds. The first thing they must do at Blockula was, that they must deny all, and devote themselves body and soul to the Devil, and promise to serve him faithfully, and confirm all this with an oath (initiation). Hereupon they cut their fingers (Odinism), and with their blood write their name in his book (Revelations). They added that he caused them to be baptized, too, by such priests as he had there (Antichrist's Sacraments).

And he, the Devil, bids them believe that the day of judgment will come speedily, and therefore sets them on work to build a great house of stone (Babel), promising that in that house he will preserve them from God's fury, and cause them to enjoy the greatest delights and pleasures (Moslem). But while they work exceeding hard at it, there falls a great part of the wall down again.

They said, they had seen sometimes a very great Devil like a Dragon, with fire round about him, and bound with an iron chain (Apocalyptic), and the Devil that converses with them tells them that if they confess anything he will let that great Devil loose upon them, whereby all Sweedeland shall come into great danger.

They added that the Devil had a church there, such another as in the town of Mohra. When the Commissioners were coming he told the Witches they should not fear them; for he would certainly kill them all. And they confessed that some of them had attempted to murder the Commissioners, but had not been able to effect it.

Some of the children talked much of a white Angel (Frigga as christian tutelary), which used to forbid them what the Devil had bid them do, and told them that those doings should not last long. What had been done had been permitted because of the wickedness of the people.

Those of Elfdale confessed that the Devil used to play upon a harp before them (Tannhauser), and afterwards to go with them that he liked best into a chamber, when he committed venerous acts with them (Asmodeus); and this indeed all confessed, that he had carnal knowledge of them, and that the Devil had sons and daughters by them, which he did marry together, and they . . . brought forth toads and serpents (Echidna).

After this they sat down to table, and those that the Devil esteemed most were placed nearest to him; but the children must stand at the door, where he himself gives them meat and drink (Sacrament). After meals they went to dancing, and in the meanwhile swore and cursed most dreadfully, and afterwards went to fighting one with another (Valhalla).

They also confessed that the Devil gives them a beast about the bigness and shape of a young cat (Hecate), which they call a carrier; and that he gives them a bird as big as a raven (Odin's messenger), but white; and these two creatures they can send anywhere, and wherever they come they take away all sorts of victuals they can get, butter, cheese, milk, bacon, and all sorts of seeds, whatever they find, and carry it to the witch. What the bird brings they may keep for themselves, but what the carrier brings they must reserve for the Devil, and that is brought to Blockula, where he doth give them of it so much as he thinks fit. They added likewise that these carriers fill themselves to full sometimes, that they are forced to spue ('Odin's booty') by the way, which spuing is found in several gardens, where colworts grow, and not far from the houses of these witches. It is of a yellow colour like gold, and is called butter of witches.

The Lords Commissioners were indeed very earnest, and took great pains to persuade them to show some of their tricks, but to no purpose; for they did all unanimously confess that since they had confessed all, they found that all their witchcraft was gone, and that the Devil at this time appeared to them very terrible, with claws on his hands and feet, and with horns on his head, a long tail behind, and showed to them a pit burning, with a hand put out; but the Devil did thrust the person down again with an iron fork; and suggested to the witches that if they continued in their confession, he would deal with them in the same manner.

The ministers of both Elfdale and Mohra were the chief inciters of this investigation, and both testified that they had suffered many tortures in the night from the wiches. One was taken by the throat and so violently used that 'for some weeks he was not able to speak or perform divine service.'

WHITE AND BLACK MAGIC

Dennis Wheatley

The Devil is just round the corner, and he is watching you. Don't you believe that? There are a lot of people who do, and some of them, even in this country, still participate in abominable rites for the purpose of courting his favour.

If you do not believe that the Devil is interested in you, then you do not believe in God, without Whose knowledge, so the Bible tells us, not a sparrow falls. You cannot believe in one and not the other.

In the beginning Lucifer, to give the Devil his personal name, was an Archangel. His pride and ambition caused him to become the leader of the first revolution. God gave St. Michael command of the loyal angels. There was a tremendous battle and Michael's angels drove Lucifer and his angels out of Heaven *down to Earth*. That is why the Devil is known as 'The Lord of This World'.

That, too, is why, when our Lord Jesus Christ was on earth, the Devil was able to take Him up into a High Place and offer Him dominion over the fair cities and fruitful plains. To deny that the Temptation occurred is to deny a fundamental tenet of the Christian religion.

In the Middle Ages it was not uncommon for people to report that the Devil had appeared to them. In those days everyone's mind was dominated by religion. Most people attended two services on Sundays, fasted on Fridays and were present at family prayers morning and evening. They had no holidays other than Saints' days and going on a pilgrimage; they went regularly to confession and, for even the smallest sin, had to perform a penance. For them Heaven and Hell were vivid realities and, as life was cheap, they might find themselves pitchforked into one or the other with little warning. So it is not surprising that the more imaginative sometimes 'saw things'. We may, therefore, put down most of these reported 'visions' as the product of an empty stomach upon an empty brain. But not all.

Not, that is, if we can believe the late Aleister Crowley,

who once assured me that it is perfectly possible to raise – he did not say the Devil, but that was what he meant.

Of course, it is not suggested that the mighty Lucifer – who is second only in power to the Lord God Himself – appears to people in person. But each of us has a Guardian Angel, and it is his opposite number, a creature of the Devil's charged with our undoing, who, in exceptional circumstances, may become visible to human eyes.

The form in which such evil entities materialise is naturally that expected of them. Hence the fire-breathing horrors with horns, cloven hoofs and spiked tail which appeared to people in the Middle Ages, and that in Crowley's case it was that of Pan – the coldly evil Greek horned-god whom he had deliberately conjured up.

Why, you may ask, are people rarely troubled by such supernatural visitors in these days? The answer is that life is infinitely more complex, and the modern mind occupied by such things as politics, sport, the cinema, travel, broadcasts, the constant change in the fashions of clothes, and so on – to *the exclusion of religion*. They are no longer interested in either saints or demons.

But do not suppose that, for that reason, the Devil no longer exists. As part of the original Creation he is immortal. Being no fool he has adapted himself to modern conditions and gone underground.

It is with good reason that one of his names is 'Lord of Misrule'. God's wish, clearly manifested in the teachings of Jesus Christ, is that we should avoid all cause for quarrels – and so lead *peaceful, orderly lives*. The Devil's province is to make us do the opposite. By luring individuals into sin he can break up families; by fostering trade disputes he can cause conditions which ultimately lead to poverty and crime; by arousing the passions of nations he can cause war.

From the beginning of time he has made tools of the greedy, the discontented and the ambitious, stimulating them by the temptation of power to sabotage peace, prosperity and good stable government. Can anyone maintain that he has been idle during the past half century?

These subtle and ubiquitous activities apart, the Devil still plays an active role in the lives of quite a number of people. It is a fact that any day in a bus or a train you may be sitting opposite to a man or woman who has made a pact with Satan, or been sold to him.

In the introduction to Story IV 'A Life for a Life' I have already mentioned the case of the Essex woman who was sold as a child to the Devil; and as 'Lord of this World' the Devil does not, of course, confine his attention to Christian people. As an example there is the case of the young Australian aboriginal, Lyn Wulumu, which was recently featured in the Press.

His mother-in-law wanted him out of the way so she 'sung him the song of the dreamtime snake'. When this is done by a votary of Satan a dream-snake coils itself round the body of the victim and gradually *crushes* him until he can no longer breathe. Lyn Wulumu, unquestionably a dying man, was flown down by the Methodist Mission to Darwin Hospital. Four doctors could find nothing whatever wrong with him physically, but they put him in an iron lung; his life was saved and it is now reported that he has regained the will to live.

My books with occult backgrounds have brought me many hundreds of letters from all parts of the world upon similar subjects. Scores of them are, of course, from people with bees in their bonnets; but with some knowledge of such matters it is not difficult to sort the wheat from he chaff, and many are from doctors, magistrates and clergymen – vouching for their personal knowledge of happenings impossible to explain except as the result of witchcraft.

The fact is that, although unrealized by most Europeans, in *every* great city, in the jungles of Africa, the villages of Asia, the plantations of the West Indies, and even in some remote hamlets of our own countryside. Satanism is still practised.

The dual principle of Good and Evil, which is the basis of every religion, must continue in perpetual conflict until the end of time. On the Right hand we have light, warmth, growth and order; on the Left hand, darkness, cold, decay and chaos.

Each of us, having within us a part of the eternal Spirit, is able at will to communicate with the Higher Powers and draw down from them additional power to ourselves. The Saints did so by prayer to God, which enabled them to perform their miracles. The Devil may be found even quicker to answer.

As a young officer in the 1914–18 war, while convalescing, I played a lot of *vingt-et-un*. After one ten-hour session, having become bored from drawing few cards worth betting upon, on the bank passing to me, I called on the Devil to give me luck. I drew two aces, doubled the table, drew another ace, split three times and finished with two naturals and a five and under. Everyone paid me sixteen times his original stake.

That shook the other chaps at the table; but it shook me infinitely more, as, sooner or later, that sort of 'luck' has to be paid for.

I have never prayed to the Devil since. Neither have I ever attended any form of magical ceremony or a séance. It is obviously such a fascinating game that even the strongest-willed person could easily get drawn further and further into it until — well, there are several very real dangers. The least is that one might find oneself being black-mailed for taking part in obscene practices. The worst, failure to pull out in time, with the realization that one had imperilled one's immortal soul. There is also the risk of slipping up in some ritual, with consequent failure to keep under control the forces one has called up. The result of that used to be called demonic possession. It is now classed as lunacy. One of Crowley's occult 'operations' misfired; so that he was found next morning a gibbering idiot, and had to spend six months in an asylum.

By prayer, fasting, and mortification of the flesh, the Saints called down power in order that they might perform miracles to the glorification of God, and heal the sick. This, the use of Supernatural Power for good or *unselfish ends*, is WHITE MAGIC.

The use of Supernatural Power for wicked or *selfish ends* is BLACK MAGIC. Such magic is of the Devil and can be obtained only by such sexual depravity and bestial rites as are described in the official reports of the initiation cere-monies of the Mau Mau.

Yet it is not only in Africa that such abominations are practised. A few years ago women were giving themselves up to hideous eroticism with a great carved ebony figure, during Satanic orgies held in a secret temple in Bayswater, London, W.2.

THE BLACK ART AND THE SUPERNATURAL

Dennis Wheatley

Perhaps the most interesting man I met while collecting data for my novels with occult backgrounds was Mr. Rollo Ahmed. He was an advanced practitioner of Yoga and made good use of it. Although a native of the West Indies he never wore an overcoat and used to go about London in the winter in a thin cotton suit. One night, when it was well below freezing, he arrived to dine with me. He had no gloves but his hands were as warm as toast.

Rollo Ahmed was deeply versed in magical lore and possessed the gift of explaining it with great lucidity. From him I learnt much of the theory of the Black Art. Briefly it may be defined as a system of short cuts to obtaining Power.

Anyone can say prayers, or think evil. God will give new strength and fortitude in answer to prayer. The Devil will give strength and resolution actually to perform the evil deed contemplated. However, the human brain resembles a radio set. It needs tuning in to get the best results.

In very early times ways were discovered of 'tuning in' more rapidly. The holy used fasting and mortification of the flesh; the unholy gross indulgence and sexual depravity. Hence the wild orgies which are a main feature of every Satanic gathering – both ancient and modern.

It was also found that contact could be more swiftly achieved by the use of certain material aids. For example, the Clairvoyant does not actually see things in the crystal. It is a device to induce self-hypnotism and turn the mind inward so that it can pick up occult vibrations. To achieve this state practitioners of the Black Art consume potions composed of the vilest secretions of the human body. The Mau Mau do this; so, too, do the depraved followers of the Devil's cult who still live in our midst. Such acts may be compared to the ringing of a bell which summons a supernatural Power.

SUPERNATURAL is simply a word to express that which lies beyond our comprehension, and MAGIC the procuring of a result normally regarded as impossible by the accepted

LAWS of cause and effect. In the MATERIAL sphere the MAGIC of yesterday becomes the SCIENCE of today; but there remain innumerable NATURAL LAWS which are not yet generally understood. That applies particularly to the ability of certain humans to call upon forces of a SPIRITUAL nature; and since all spiritual power emanates from either God or the Devil those who employ them become priests and priestesses of either Good or Evil.

The good 'priest' uses supernatural power for unselfish ends; and the most common forms of his activities are 'pain-taking' and faith healing. A recent inquiry by the British Medical Association has revealed that this type of White Magic is widely practised all over Britain. The investigators admit that warts can be *charmed* away, and can offer no explanation for that. Concerning more important cures, brought about by prolonged prayer, their report states:

'In the Committee's opinion it is probably better to acknowledge that the cures are at present inexplicable on scientific grounds.'

In this connection I had first-hand knowledge of an extra-ordinary happening while staying with my sister-in-law in South Africa. Her old negro cook, Maria, complained of acute pains in the breast and displayed to her an ugly tumour. Maria was at once taken down to the hospital. After examining her, the doctor put her in the waiting-room then, just outside its door, told my sister-in-law that the tumour was an advanced cancer and that it must be cut out without delay. An hour later he telephoned to ask where Maria was. She had disappeared.

Ten days later she returned with not a trace of the tumour. When asked for an explanation she said: 'I hears what that white doctor says to you, Missis, 'bout cuttin' me up. I's scared, so I slips off back to ma Kraal. The black doctor, he throws the bones for me and I's well again now.'

Another supernatural potential of the human mind which has now been recognized by the medical profession is Hypno-tism. Yet no doctor can explain how it is possible for a subject to be made so iron rigid that his neck can be placed on one chair-back, his feet on another, and the hypnotist be able to kneel on the subject's stomach without his body even bending.

The French psychologist, Pierre Janet, has even succeeded in hypnotising a patient at a distance of over a mile, at a time known only to the experimenters. That brings us to Mental Telepathy, of which countless people have had personal experience. Such happenings used to be put down to coincidence; but a few years ago Dr. Soal, by infinitely patient and prolonged tests, proved the case for telepathy conclusively. And Water Divining – a common and valuable practice – what explanation can science give for that?

Turning to more sensational manifestations of the supernatural, many people have been saved from death by warnings of an occult nature. One of the most intriguing is that which was vouched for by the late Lord Dufferin and Ava.

While staying in a house in Ireland, one night before getting into bed he looked out of the window. Below him in the bright moonlight he saw a man carrying a coffin. The man looked up; his face was striking and most unpleasant. Next morning no one in the house could offer any explanation of this extraordinary occurrence. Years later, Lord Dufferin was in Paris. He was about to enter an already crowded hotel lift. Suddenly he recognized the face of the lift attendant as that of the ghoul with the coffin. Startled, he stepped back. The man slammed the lift gates and up went the lift. At the third floor the cable broke. It crashed to the basement and everyone in it, including the lift man, was killed.

Many people will swear to having seen a ghost; but proof of the actual materialization of a spirit is very difficult to obtain. Personally, I am prepared to take the word of that great seeker after Truth, Harry Price. He carried out countless tests of reported psychic phenomena and ruthlessly exposed scores of fake mediums; but he told me once that there could be no possible explanation, other than a supernatural one, for the appearances of Rosalie.

Every conceivable check to prevent fraud was taken. Yet on using his luminous plaque he saw this little naked girl standing in front of him; and having felt her all over would have sworn – but for the low temperature of her flesh – to her being a living child.

It was Harry Price who told me of a strange haunting in Sussex. One bedroom in this old house was so badly haunted that even the most sceptical visitors woke in it to find themselves being strangled; and any food left in a semi-basement room became putrid within a few hours. An exorcist was called in. The exorcism was carried out just before dawn in the bedroom. A ball, seemingly composed of black smoke and about the size of a football, appeared, rolled downstairs, out through the window of the semi-basement room and across the lawn to disappear in a small lake. The lake was later dredged and no less than three skeletons were brought up from it.

The Reverend Montague Summers told me of an exorcism he had performed in Ireland. He was called to a farmer's wife who, it was said, was possessed by an evil spirit. He arrived in the evening. On the table in the living-room the remains of a cold leg of mutton had already been placed for supper; the woman was in the same room. At the sight of a priest she became so violent that she had to be held down. As he sprinkled the Holy Water on her and commanded the demon to come forth, a small cloud of black smoke issued from her foam-flecked mouth. It went straight into the cold mutton, and within a few minutes everyone present saw that the meat was alive with maggots.

Few men had more knowledge of the Occult than Montague Summers, and his books upon Witchcraft and Were-wolves are classics. But he was, to say the least of it, a curious character. Rumour has it that he was not, in fact, a priest.

My wife and I went to stay at his house for a weekend. On the ceiling of our bedroom we found a score of enormous spiders. When I mentioned this, he replied only, 'I like spiders'; and in his garden my wife came upon the biggest toad she has ever seen. He tried to sell me a rare book. When I refused to buy it, I have never seen such malefic anger come into the eyes of any man. We made an excuse to leave on Sunday morning.

With his long silver locks and, normally, benign expression, he looked like a Restoration Bishop. Years later I used his physical appearance for Canon Copely-Syle in *To the Devil – a Daughter*. For that I had a precedent, as in Mr. Somerset Maugham's early book *The Magician* the sorcerer, Hado, bears a striking resemblance to Aleister Crowley.

Mentioning books reminds me of A. E. W. Mason's *Prisoner in the Opal*. In it, he rightly associates the presence of the most powerful evil entities with intense cold. Dante's lowest circle in Hell was formed of ice.

I do not regard myself as psychic but I have once felt that terrifying chill. I was building a shack by moonlight in an old walled garden behind the Somme battlefield. It came upon me without rhyme or reason. I *knew* that something incredibly evil was watching me from behind – and it had suddenly become very cold. After a minute that seemed an eternity I panicked and fled in abject terror.

All this adds up to the fact that one cannot laugh off the Supernatural, and that like everything else in the Universe it is governed by definite laws. To utilise those laws for personal ends is to practise the Black Art. And it is still practised in England today.

One of the doctors who gave evidence before the B.M.A. Committee of Inquiry into faith healing stated that Black as well as White Magic is still widely practised in Devonshire; and that among his patients *he had had one definite death caused by Witchcraft*. That is something to give pause for thought to those readers who will this summer be motoring through Devon's lovely lanes.

THE WITCHES' SABBATH

Dennis Wheatley

The Sabbath – at which thirteen persons met by night to worship the Devil with obscene rites – was in Europe the direct outcome of the spread of Christianity. The New religion sought to enforce fasting, chastity and a generally puritanical existence. Many people were used to looking forward to such Roman festivals as the Saturnalia, when slaves were for a day the equal of their masters, and feasting ended in a general orgy. In consequence the Old religion went underground.

It must, too, be remembered that in the Dark Ages there were no buses to take people from lonely villages into the towns; no newspapers, football pools or television. So the Devil was on a good wicket for tempting country folk into occasional nights of wild indulgence.

Today Sabbaths – like those recently reported from Birmingham – usually take place in houses. But one cannot altogether ignore the persistent rumours of moonlight gatherings for Satan worship in Cornwall, Derbyshire and Northern Scotland; and there is very good reason to believe that a Sabbath was held on the site of an old pagan temple in the Cotswolds as recently as last April.

Aleister Crowley, so I was told by a well-known Member of Parliament who knew him intimately, held a Sabbath, of sorts, when he was up at Cambridge. He was a brilliant scholar, and planned to produce a Greek play; but owing to its immorality the Master of John's forbade him to do so. To be avenged he made a wax image of the Master, then induced some of his fellow students to accompany him on a propitious night to a field. Having performed certain rites, Crowley called on the Devil and was about to plunge a needle into the liver of the wax figure. But his companions panicked. His arm was jerked and, instead, the figure's ankle was pierced. Next day the Master fell down some steps and broke his ankle.

Covens always numbered thirteen – a parody of The Last Supper. They met in lonely dells, or sometimes in a high place if upon it there was an ancient monolith. There had to be a pond near-by : if there were not the members of the Coven dug a hole and urinated into it.

Sabbaths were held at full-moon, and on St. Walburga's Eve (April 30th), St. John's Eve (June 23rd) and All-hallowe'en (October 31st). On those dates Grand Sabbaths were also held, by thirteen Covens uniting at such places as the Brocken mountain in Germany and on Salisbury Plain.

The badge of office of the Chief of each Coven was a string worn below the left knee. This emblem of occult power goes back to prehistoric times, and it is probable that the Most Noble Order of the Garter originated from it.

The chronicle tells us that while King Edward III was dancing with his mistress, the Countess of Salisbury, her garter fell off; and, to her great confusion, snatching it up, he proclaimed the founding of the Order. Her confusion *would* have been great if it was a witch's garter; and it is conceivable that she was the Queen Witch of England. If so, by seizing her insignia he took her power to himself. It may well have been a clever political move to merge into his person as King the Chieftainship of the followers of the Old religion, of whom in those days there were still great numbers.

It is at least curious that he should have limited the Order to the Sovereign, the Prince of Wales and 24 Knights – two Covens; and that the Sovereign's mantle is embroidered with 168 garters which, with the garter he wears, makes 169 – i.e. 13 × 13 signifying lordship over that number of Covens.

The attempted suppression of the Old religion did not start till much later, and had its origin in the growing Puritanism which led to the Reformation. There then began the horrible witch-hunts in which old women, often guilty only of ugliness or practising White Magic, were ducked in ponds to see if they would float, stripped and searched for a third teat from which they were believed to feed their familiars – a cat, owl or toad – and stuck with pins, to find the spot rendered painless by the touch of the Devil's finger when he had accepted them as his own.

When preparing for a Sabbath, witches smeared their bodies with an unguent. Some unguents had stupefying qualities which caused them to *dream* that they had ridden naked through the night on a broomstick and that the Devil had had sexual intercourse with them.

The cult of the Voodoo goddess Erzulie is of a similar nature. Today, in the West Indies, every Thursday night thousands of negroes light candles to her, put clean sheets on their beds and – as she is violently jealous – turn their unfortunate wives out of the house; then give themselves up to dream embraces with this female counterpart of Satan.

The use of unguents by those who actually attended the Sabbaths is paralleled by modern worshippers in Satanic Temples inhaling the smoke from burning certain herbs. This has the effect of overcoming the scruples of the more timid, who might otherwise be revolted by the acts they are called on to perform, and stimulating the more hardened to a frenzy of abandonment. Aphrodisiacs are, of course, taken by all to increase sexual potency.

A Sabbath must have been a truly hellish spectacle. Head masks of goats, bats, cats and other animals were worn to conceal the identity of the participants. In a great cauldron a hell-broth bubbled – 'eye of newt and toe of frog, wool of bat and tongue of dog', etc. A band struck up but each member of it played a different tune, resulting in cacophony. Grabbing up food and drink, the company gorged themselves to a surfeit. Naked but for their masks, they danced in a circle back to back. The Chief of the Coven presented his posterior and the others kissed it in homage. He, or she, then 'blessed' evil amulets, among which there was sometimes a dead man's hand – a talisman that was said to enable a robber to enter any house without being heard. Finally, in a wild orgy they vied with one another in sexual excess and every form of perversion.

The equivalents of Sabbaths are held by the Mau Mau to initiate recruits. Among other horrors the initiate, male or female, is made to perform most bestial acts with a goat – and one of the Devil's names is 'The Goat of Mendes'.

In Haiti, too, such abominations still take place. There, the most terrible rite ever conceived is performed – the taking of a man's soul. The selected victim is bewitched and to all appearances dies. After he has been buried his body is dug up and re-animated. He does not know who he is; his memory has been completely obliterated. He has become a Zombie. The wizard who has stricken him puts him to work in the fields. There he labours automatically and tirelessly, day after day, until he really dies from natural causes.

Zora Huston, a coloured American journalist of repute, carried out an exhaustive investigation into this subject. In her book, *Voodoo Gods*, she publishes a photograph of a Zombie.

THE BLACK MASS

Dennis Wheatley

Witches' Sabbaths, in various forms, are still held by people of every race and religion, but the Black Mass is exclusively a perversion of Christianity. It is a religious ceremony as distinct from a Satanic 'beanfeast'.

Each Holy Mass is dedicated to a definite 'intention'; so are Black Masses. It will be recalled that King Albert I of Belgium died in most mysterious circumstances. He was an exceptionally good man, so his premature end was a tragedy for all Europe. Soon after the publication of my book *The Haunting of Toby Jugg* I received a letter from a woman who stated that she had been present at a Black Mass held in Brighton the day before King Albert died, and that it had been held *with the intention of bringing about his death*. Her account was highly circumstantial and showed her to have a thorough knowledge of the Black Art.

Incidentally, it was at Brighton that Aleister Crowley was cremated in 1947, and the Black Magic rites that his disciples performed at his funeral led to an inquiry by the Town Council.

The mummery indulged in during the celebration of a Black Mass might seem rather childish, were it not so horrible and carried out *with intense seriousness* by those who participate. It is a complete travesty of the Christian ritual and the supreme act in the worship of the Devil.

The celebrant and his assistant – who is always a woman – wear their vestments back to front, and hitched up so as to expose their sexual parts. The altar is furnished with a broken crucifix standing upside down, and black candles in which brimstone has been mixed with the tallow. The ceremony opens by the congregation reciting the Lord's Prayer backwards.

Of this particular blasphemy I was an unconscious witness three years ago in a cellar Night Club in Nice. The compère of the cabaret was a haggard-looking man of about sixty, with a shock of white hair. After a husky rendering of some questionable songs, he began to intone. My French

148

is limited almost to reading a restaurant menu, so I asked the friends who had brought me there what he was saying.

'The *Paternoster* backwards,' they replied, shrugging it off as a memory feat in ill taste. But my own belief is that it was a subtle form of 'invitation' – an indication to anyone present who was interested in Black Magic that the blasphemer could put them in touch with a Satanic Circle.

A more usual means of recruiting for the Devil is through Spiritualism. I cannot believe that any good ever comes of trying to get in touch with loved ones who have died, although one cannot blame broken-hearted people who attempt to do so; but others attend séances only in search of excitement. At many séances the Black fraternity have what might be termed 'talent scouts'. They are on the lookout for widows 'of a certain age', for wealthy gentlemen in the fifties who have developed a prostate, and for young women who show signs of being neurotic.

They tell such people that the medium's 'act' is kindergarten stuff, and that they can show them something really thrilling. The older ones of both sexes who accept such invitations soon find their desires satisfied – at the price of having been photographed by hidden cameras and later blackmailed – the younger, drugged, dragooned and terrified, become the unpaid prostitutes of the Satanic Temples – from which hideous bondage they rarely manage to escape.

At a Black Mass the whole ritual is recited backwards, then Communion wafers are defiled. These wafers are stolen from churches, and during the past twenty years the Press has reported numerous cases of such thefts. Next the sacrifice is offered up, its throat cut, the blood caught in a chalice and drunk in place of Communion wine. Finally the celebrant has intercourse with his assistant on the altar and the congregation, made frenzied by incense containing drugs, throw themselves upon one another in a general orgy.

To be of maximum effectiveness the Black Mass should be celebrated by an unfrocked priest, and the sacrifice be an unweaned babe. Madame de Montespan, the beautiful mistress of Louis XIV, ordered many Black Masses with the 'intention' of retaining the King's waning love; and, it is said, both gave herself to the infamous Abbé Guibourg, who celebrated them for her, and bought unwanted babies for sacrifice.

The case of the warrior-sorcerer Gilles de Rais – upon whom the Blue Beard story was founded – permits of no doubt. After his execution the remains of 140 murdered children were found in the dungeons of his castle.

In our modern world it is not easy to buy infants, or kidnap them without risk of detection; so the usual sacrifice is a cat. Aleister Crowley, so a disciple of his told me, always used cats at his Abbaye de Thelême in Sicily. There was, too, the severed paw of a white kitten left on the altar of the Church of St. John the Baptist at Yarcombe, Somerset, in 1948. The church had been broken into and desecrated in various ways, making it evident that a Black Mass had been celebrated there.

The parallel Pagan rituals of the Carthaginians, the Aztecs and the Druids, all called for human sacrifice, but not necessarily of a child. And there remains unsolved the murder of Charles Walton at Meon Hill, Warwickshire, in 1945, to which no explanation could be found – other than that it was a ritual killing.

THE DEVIL'S SECRET SOCIETIES

Dennis Wheatley

'They draw pentacles on the floor, sir, and late at night the men dress up in silk smocks with the signs of the Zodiac on them. The ladies come down wearing masks and red, high-heeled shoes. I've seen black candles, too.

'I hadn't an idea what it was all about. Just thought they were playing charades, or something, until I read your book *To the Devil – a Daughter*. Of course, I tumbled to it then. There can be no doubt about it, my employers are Satanists.'

The above is from a letter written to me by a chauffeur. He was employed by wealthy people who lived in a big house in the Eastern Counties. He went on to say that these parties sometimes numbered as many as twenty people, some of whom came down from London in big cars and drove off in them again before dawn.

This man wrote to me three times. He gave his address, signed his name and offered to meet me in his nearest town. In view of that, and the fact that his letters showed no signs of hysteria, I see no reason to suppose that he was not telling the truth.

Such gatherings to practise the Black Art undoubtedly take place. There are, of course, phony imitations, organized only for the purpose of lechery followed by blackmail, but genuine Satan worship is still as prevalent today as – shall we say – the dope traffic.

Magic is a science. It cannot just be picked up. One would have to have a quite exceptional brain to make, unaided, any practical use of Eliphas Levi's *Doctrine and Ritual of Transcendental Magic*, or the famous *Malleus Maleficarum*, or even of Aleister Crowley's *Magick in Theory and Practice*; let alone of the rare but great classics such as *Le Clavicule de Salomon* and *Grimoire of Pope Honorius*.

Without a sound understanding of the esoteric doctrine it would be futile – if not actually dangerous – to call up evil forces, or to rely for protection on a pentacle the Cabalistic signs of which had been chosen by guesswork.

It follows that the sorcerer or witch must be taught his or

her business, just as the priests of any other religion are taught theirs. Therefore, secret societies to hand down the Devil's mysteries, and to spread his cult as widely as possible among the ignorant, have always existed.

Their most successful operations have been to infiltrate themselves into the leadership of movements for reform. Many saintly men have led revolts against the abuses of the Church, but their words have been misinterpreted and their work worse than undone by the disciples of evil a generation later.

An example is cited in the first volume of Sir Winston Churchill's book, *A History of the English-Speaking Peoples*. The Albigenses, a people who in the thirteenth century inhabited a large part of south-western France, were led to believe that 'life on this earth in the flesh was the work of Satan', which meant that 'they were freed from the menaces of the next'. Like a prairie fire immorality and disorder spread through the whole region. The King of France launched a 'home Crusade'; they were massacred by the thousand, until none was left.

Then there were the Knights Templar, an Order of Chivalry founded for the rescue of the Holy Sepulchre. Their main base was Malta. In their decadence, perverted by evil successors to their early Grand Masters, initiates had to spit three times on the Cross and swear allegiance to the Devil in the form of a bearded idol named Baphomet.

Their headquarters in Paris was a palace-fortress called the Temple. King Philippe IV had their Grand Master, Jacques de Molay, and many of his Knights arrested there, and brought to trial for heresy. They were burnt at the stake. But the Order swore to be avenged upon the Monarchy of France.

Five hundred years later it was. From the tower of the Temple Louis XVI was taken to the guillotine. And that the Temple had been chosen for his prison *was not chance*. The French Revolution was directed by the Masonic Lodge of the Grand Orient, which had inherited the championship of evil.

It should be clearly understood that Masonry in the British Commonwealth has no connection whatever with the Grand Orient. Continental Masonry is altogether different. Its inner circles are the successors of those of the German Illuminati and the Rosicrucians – two other great secret societies whose leaders started them with good intent, but which later fell into evil hands. Even its rank and file members are avowed atheists.

In the past two hundred years the Grand Orient has brought about many revolutions and in 1902–4, with the French War Minister, General André, in its toils, it succeeded in so weakening the High Command of the Army that France would have proved incapable of resisting invasion.

It is the Grand Orient, more than all other factors together, which has reduced France, once the most powerful nation in Europe, to her present pitiful condition. But now its activities are being surpassed by those of its fellow revolutionaries and atheists – the Communists. Their founder, Karl Marx, advocated the destruction of the middle classes by every means *including violence*, and their efforts are worldwide.

The dual principle of Good and Evil, which is the basis of every religion, must continue in perpetual conflict until the end of time. On the Right hand we have warmth, light, growth and order; on the Left hand darkness, cold, decay and chaos.

Do the authorities know of any Satanic societies operating in our midst today? I can only tell you that when discussing this matter in 1938 with one of my oldest friends – a man who has spent most of his life in MI.5 – he asked me:

'Does "The Shadow" convey anything to you?'

'No,' I replied.

He made a wry grimace and said: 'Believe me, Dennis, I would rather be up against a combination of the most dangerous German and Russian agents I have ever known, than up against "The Brothers of the Shadow".'

FORETELLING THE FUTURE

Dennis Wheatley

There is a 'gap in the curtain' through which some people can see. Of that I have incontestable proof.

In the 1920s I used occasionally to visit a seer named Dewhirst. He predicted to me the circumstances in which I should meet my wife and even described the way she did her hair.

In 1932 I went to see him again. Immediately I entered his room he exclaimed : 'You've written a book !'

That was pretty staggering as I had not seen him for two years and I had only just sent the manuscript of my first novel to an agent. But he went on :

'You are on your right road at last. Someone whose name begins with H will sell millions of your books. They will be read in every country under the sun.' Then he named the seven weeks ahead, on which I would have good news about my book.

On that date I learned that Walter Hutchinson had taken The Forbidden Territory *for publication.*

He used no cards or crystal. Only lesser soothsayers require such aids for tuning in to the occult. And I have never known anyone else with such powers of supernormal vision.

Fortune-telling of this kind is not evil. But it becomes so when cruelty to animals and/or Satanic rituals are employed. The Ancients examined the entrails of still living birds and beasts; and necromancy entails raising the dead – as that dark tale in the Bible tells us the Witch of Endor did for Saul.

Whole life forecasts are obtained by casting horoscopes. That means relating the day and hour of birth to the position of the Heavenly bodies. It is a long and complicated process, as the Sun, Moon and Planets are all credited with contributing to a person's character and influencing his acts. Each, too, has a number, and every person has a number arrived at by a combination of his birth date and the numerological value of the letters forming his name. The ancient belief is that from these lucky and unlucky days and periods can be foretold.

This possibility cannot be ruled out. There is good reason to believe that plants thrive better when planted under a waxing Moon. It is possible that each Heavenly body emits something in the nature of what we now term 'cosmic rays', to which the human mind is sensitive.

If so, they are governed by Natural Laws not yet fathomed by science, and we regard predictions of this kind as supernatural only because we have no explanation for them.

Palmistry is definitely a science, although not yet accepted as such. I learned to read hands while serving as a subaltern on the Western Front. With practice anyone can tell character, talents and health tendencies from the shape of the hands, their resilience, the nails and the lines on the palms. But, *when it comes to predicting the future*, the latter must be regarded as a means of tuning in.

Disappointment and warped judgment are the price that nearly everyone pays who *seeks guidance* by having his fortune told – however innocent the means. Because, even apart from fraud, the tendency is always to interpret predictions in the sense *one would like them to mean*.

The most famous oracle of ancient times was at Delphi. In a cellar priestesses threw themselves into a trance by inhaling the smoke of burning herbs, then answered questions put to them through a crack in the ceiling. Their utterances usually contained the germ of truth, but were so cryptic that numerous Greek generals were led by them into doing the wrong thing.

The extraordinary prophecies of Nostradamus, in the sixteenth century, were so obscure that few people understood them when made; yet many of them have since been fulfilled. Among other things, he predicted that in the year 2000 Paris would finally be destroyed by fire sent down from a flock of giant man-made birds coming from the Far East. That must have sounded sheer nonsense 400 years ago. But, were I likely to live that long, you would not find me drinking a champagne cocktail in the Ritz bar there round the year 2000.

Perhaps, though, by then the Russians will be occupying Paris, and the atom-belching missiles have been despatched from an Australia which has become the home base of the British people?

It is so easy to put a wrong construction on prophecies. The stars may foretell that on Wednesday 'Something is coming your way'. It may be an old boot at your head.

And predictions can lead you into trouble. When Dewhirst foretold big money from my book for me, I might have gone on a spending spree. But it was not until a year later that I received more than an advance of £30, so I would have landed myself in a nasty mess.

The following shows how futile it is to make plans based on information received by occult means. Hitler employed the best astrologers and soothsayers that could be found in the Nazi empire, and never made a move without consulting them. Churchill, on the other hand, had no dealings with such people. All War Cabinet decisions were based upon reasoned assessments submitted by our Chiefs of Staff. Yet the British – for a year, alone – held the whole might of Germany at bay.

A few more words on Magic. No saying is less true than that 'The Devil looks after his own'. I have never yet met anyone who practised Black, or even Grey, Magic who was not hard up.

Finally : should you ever have reason to believe that you or yours have come into the orbit of malignant occult forces, do not hesitate to consult your parson or priest. They will not laugh. And should you ever be confronted with an evil manifestation, have no fear. Pray for help. It will immediately be given to you. Make the Sign of the Cross and 'thou shalt not be afraid for the terror by night'.

THE SECRET GRIMOIRE OF TURIEL

Observations and method of Invoking related with great pains and diligent research.

Retire thyself Seven Days free from all company and fast and pray from sunset to sunrise. Rise every morning at Seven of the clock, and the three days previous to the Work fast upon bread and water and humble thyself before Almighty God. Watch and pray all night before the Work.

And on the day before draw the lines of the Circle in a fair place, and let the diameter of the Circle be 9 feet. Wash thyself the same day quite clean.

Make the pentacles forthwith and provide the other things necessary, with Incensing. Then being clothed in pure Vestments and having covered the Altar and lighted the candles begin about half an hour before sunrise on the Day assigned for the Work and say with great Devotion as follows :—

First Morning Prayer:—

Almighty and Most Merciful Father I beseech Thee that Thou wilt vouchsafe favourably to hear me at this time whilst I make my humble prayer and Supplication unto Thee. I confess unto Thee O Lord Thou hast justly punished me for my manifold sins and offences but Thou hast promised at what time soever a sinner doth repent of his sins and wickedness Thou wilt pardon and forgive him and turn away the remembrance of them from before Thy face.

Purge me therefore O Lord and wash me from all my offences in the Blood of Jesus Christ that, being pure and clothed in the Vestments of Sanctity, I may bring this Work to perfection, through Jesus our Lord who liveth and reigneth with Thee in the Unity of the Holy Ghost. Amen.

Sprinkle thyself with Holy Water and say :—

Asperges me Domine hysope, et mundabor. Lavabis me et super nivem dealbabor.

Hail O Mighty God, for in Thy power alone abideth the Key to all exorcising of Principalities, Powers, Thrones, Angels and Spirits. Amen.

Then bless your Girdle, saying :—

O God Who by the breath of Thy nostrils framed Heaven and Earth and wonderfully disposed of things therein in six days, grant that this now brought to perfection by Thine unworthy servant may be by Thee blessed and receive Divine virtue, power and Influence from Thee that every thing therein contained may fully operate according to the hope and confidence of me Thine unworthy servant through Jesus Christ our Lord and Saviour. Amen.

The Blessing of the Light:—

I bless thee in the Name of the Father. O Holy, Holy Lord, God, Heaven and Earth are full of Thy Glory before Whose face there is a bright shining light forever; bless now, O Lord, I beseech Thee, these creatures of light which Thou hast given for the Kindly use of man that they, by Thee being sanctified, may not be put out or extinguished by the power, malice, or filthy darkness of the devil, but may shine forth brightly and lend their assistance to this my Work, through Jesus Christ our Lord. Amen.

Then say, 'Asperges me, etc.'

Consecration of the Sword:—

O Great God Who are the God of strength and fortitude and greatly to be feared, bless O Lord, this Instrument that it may be a terror unto the Enemy, and therewith I may fight with and overcome all phantasms and oppositions of the Enemy, through the influence and help of Thy most Holy Mighty Name, On, St. Agla, and in the Cross of Jesus Christ our only Lord. Amen.

Be thou blessed and consecrated in the Name of the Father, Son, and Holy Ghost.

Asperges me, etc.

Benediction of the Lamens (Symbols, Circles):—

O God Thou God of my Salvation I call upon Thee by the mysteries of Thy most holy Name, On, St. Agla, I worship and beseech Thee by Thy Names El, Elohim, Elohe, Zebaoth, and by Thy Mighty Name Tetragrammaton,

Saday, that Thou wilt be seen in the power and force of these Thy most holy names so written filling them with divine virtue and Influence through Jesus Christ our Lord.

Benediction of the Pentacles:—

Eternal God which, by Thy Holy Wisdom, hast caused (?) great power and virtue to lie hidden in the characters and Holy Writings of Thy Spirits and angels, and hast given unto man that with them, faithfully used, power thereby to work many things; bless these, O Lord, framed and written by the hand of me Thine unworthy servant that being filled with divine virtue and Influence by Thy Commands, O Most Holy God, they may shew forth their virtue and power to Thy praise and Glory through Jesus Christ our Lord. Amen.

I bless and consecrate you in the Name of the Father, the Son, and the Holy Ghost, the God of Abraham, Isaac, and Jacob.

Asperges me, etc.   Amen.

Benediction of the Garment:—

O Holy, blessed and Eternal Lord God Who art the God of purity and delightest that our souls should appear before Thee in clean and pure and undefiled Vestments being cleansed, blessed, and consecrated by Thee, I may put them on, being therewith clothed I may be whiter than snow both in soul and body in Thy presence this day, in and through the merit, death, and passion of our only Lord and Saviour Jesus Christ, Who liveth and reigneth with Thee in the Unity of the Holy Spirit, ever one God, world without end. The God of Abraham, Isaac and Jacob bless thee, purge thee, and make thee pure, and be thou clean in the Name of the Father, Son and Holy Ghost.   Amen.

In this Thy Holy Sign O God, I fear no evil. By Thy Holy Power, and by this Thy Holy Sign all evil doth flee.

By Thy Holy Name and Thy Power which Secret was revealed to Moses, through the Holy Names written in this Book, depart far from me all ye workers of iniquity.

Bless, O Lord, I beseech Thee, this place and drive away all evil and wickedness far from it. Sanctify and make it become meet and convenient for Thy Servant to finish and bring to pass therein his desires, through Jesus Christ our Lord, Amen.

Be thou blessed and purified in the Name of the Father, Son, and Holy Ghost. Amen.

Benediction of the Perfumes:—

The God of Abraham, the God of Isaac, the God of Jacob, bless here the creatures of these kinds that they may give forth the power of their odours so that neither the Enemy nor any false Imaginations may be able to enter into them, through our Lord Jesus Christ, to whom be honour and Glory now, henceforth, and for ever. Amen.

Sprinkle them with Holy Water, saying, 'Asperges me, Domine, etc.'

Exorcism of Fire:—

I exorcise thee, O thou creature of Fire, by Him by Whom all things are made, that forthwith thou wilt cast away every phantasm from thee that it shall not be able to do any hurt in any thing. Bless, O Lord, this creature of Fire and sanctify it, that it may be blessed to set forth the praise of Thy Holy Name that no hurt may be able to come unto me, through the virtue and defence of our Lord Jesus Christ. Amen.

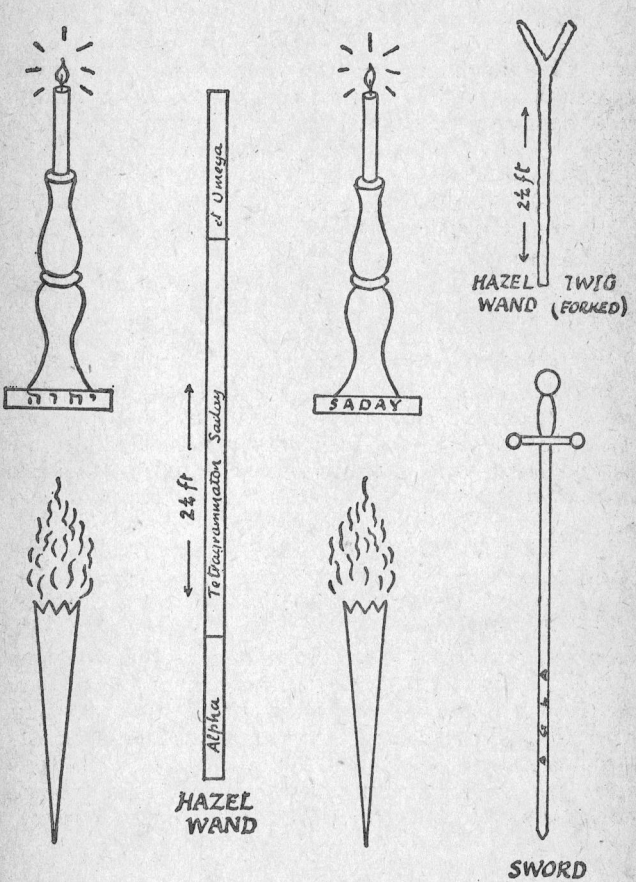

HAZEL TWIG
WAND (FORKED)

24 ft

el Omega

Saday

Te Tragrammaton

24 ft

Alpha

יהוה

SADAY

HAZEL
WAND

SWORD

AGLA

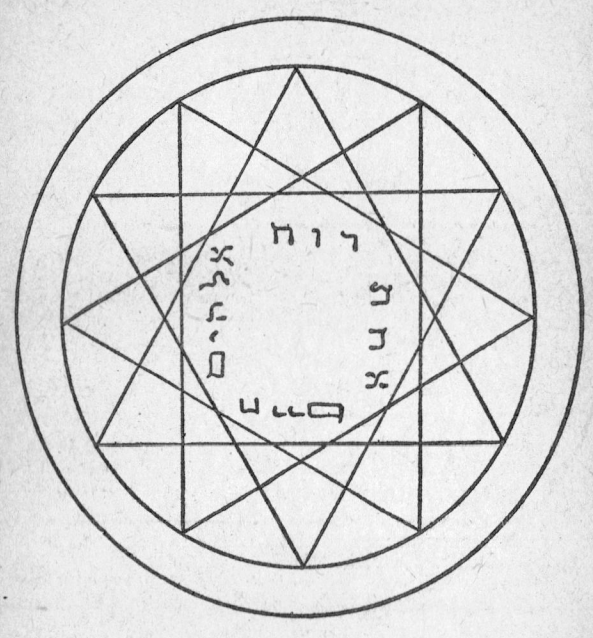

Invocation for Sunday (SOL):—

Come, Heavenly Spirits who have the effulgent rays of the Sun, Luminous Spirits who are ready to obey the power of the great Tetragrammaton, come and assist me in the operation that I am making under the auspices of the Grand Light of Day which the Eternal Creator hath formed for the use of universal nature. I invoke you for these purposes. Be favourable and auspicious to what I shall ask in the Name of Amioram, Adonai, Sabaoth.

Invocation for Monday (MOON):—

Haste ye Sublime and Intelligent Genii who are obedient
to the Sovereign Arcana, come and assist me in the operation
that I undertake under the auspices of the Grand Luminary
of the Night. I invoke you to this end and implore you to be
favourable and hear my entreaties in the Name of Him
Who commands the spirits of the Four Quarters of the
Universal Mansions : Inhabit, Bileth, Mizabu, Abinzaba.

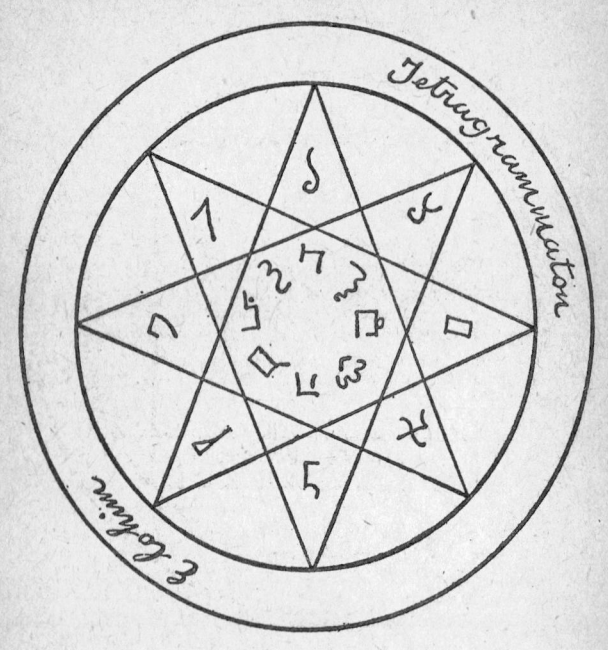

Invocation for Tuesday (MARS):—

Come Children of the Red Genii who have executed the order of the Sovereign Master of the Universe upon the armies of the rash Sennacherib, come and assist me in the operation that I undertake under the auspices of the third brilliant luminary of the firmament; be favourable to my entreaties in the Name of Adonay Sabaoth.

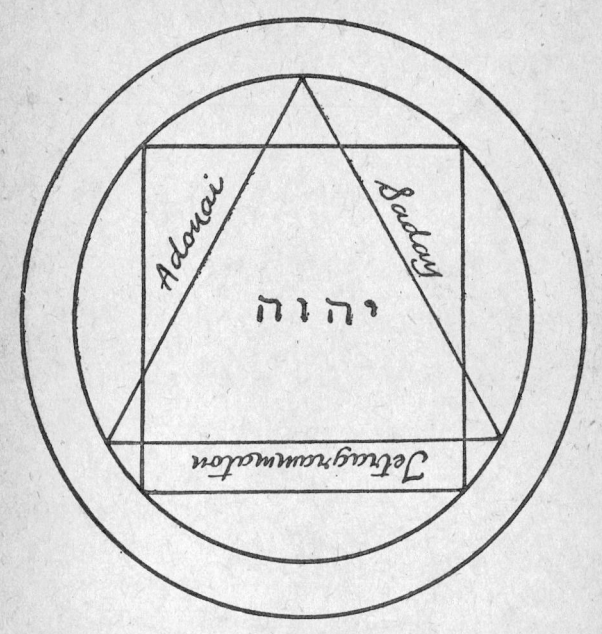

Invocation for Wednesday (MERCURY):—

Run to me with speed, come to me ye Spirits of Mercury who preside over the operation of this day, hear favourably the present invocation that I make to you under the Divine Names of Venoel, Uranel, be kind and ready to second my undertakings. Render them efficacious.

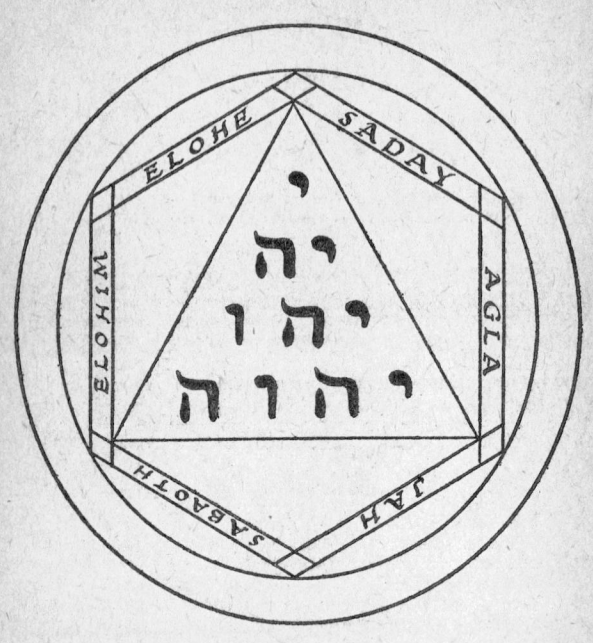

Invocation for Thursday (JUPITER):—

Come speedily ye Olepid Spirits who preside over the operation of this day. Come, Incomprehensible Zebarel and all your legions, haste to my assistance and be propitious to my undertakings, be kind and refuse me not your powerful aid and assistance.

Invocation for Friday (VENUS):—

Come on the wings of the wind, ye happy Genii who preside over the workings of the heart. Come in the Name of the Great Tetragrammaton; hear favourably the Invocation that I make this day, destined to the wonder of love. Be ready to lend me your assistance to succeed in what I have undertaken under the hope that you will be favourable to me.

Invocation for Saturday (SATURN):—

Come out of your gloomy solitude ye Saturnine spirits, come with your cohort, come with diligence to the place where I am going to begin my operation under your auspices; be attentive to my labours and contribute your assistance that it may rebound to the honour and glory of the Highest.

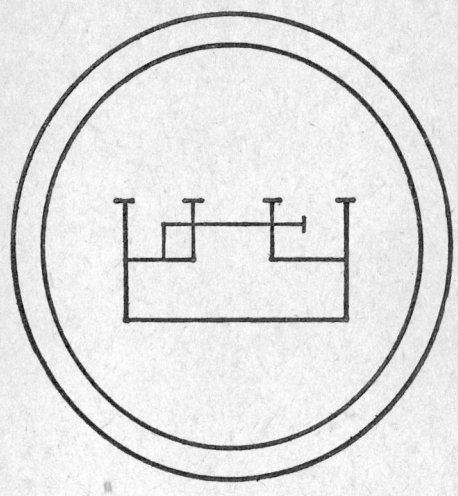

CHARACTER OF ARATRON LORD OF SATURN

Perfumes:—

Saffron, with the wood of Aloes, the Elder and the Pine. Add to it a grain of Musk, and consecrate the whole, pulverized and mixed together in a paste.

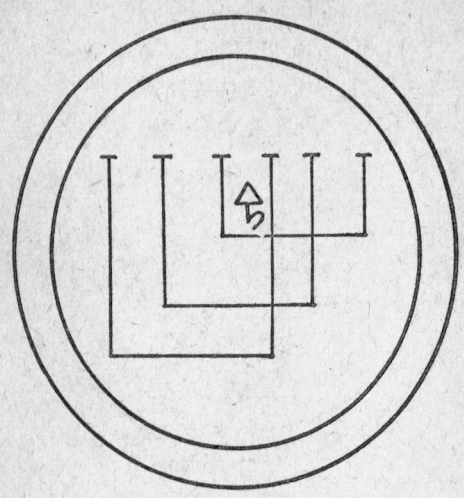

CHARACTER OF PHALEG LORD OF MARS

Perfumes:—

The head of a frog, the Bovine Blood, a grain of White Poppy, Flowers of Camomile, and Camphor, pulverized into a paste by the mixing of the blood of a Virgin Kid.

Footnote:—

On this and subsequent occasions when the use of blood or parts of animals is specified we have retained the wording of the original MS. for the sake of authenticity. We would, however, remark that in the opinion of experienced occultists the use of blood is neither desirable nor essential, being apt to have a bad effect upon the operator. It is suggested that the white of a new-laid egg would prove an effective substitute, having a similar life potential, and being equally suitable as a cohesive medium.

EDITOR

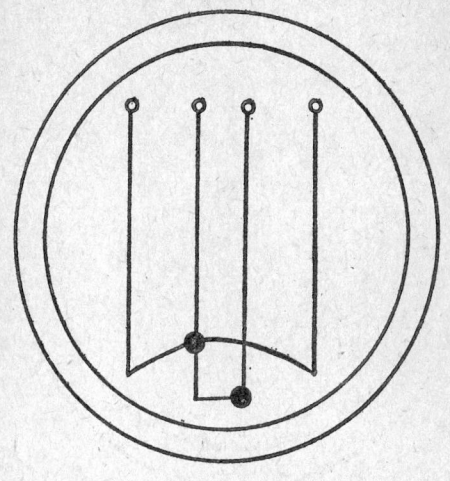

CHARACTER OF PHUL LORD OF THE MOON

Perfumes:—

Leaves of the Mandrake, Sal Ammonia, Roots of Gentian, Valerian herbs finely cut, a little Sulphur, made into a paste with the blood of a black Cat.

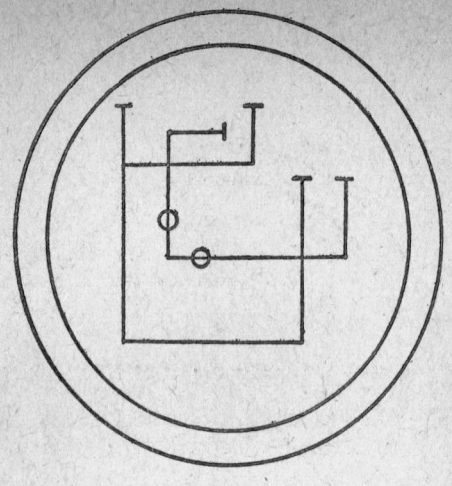

CHARACTER OF BETHOR LORD OF JUPITER

Perfumes:—

Sandalwood of the East, leaves of Agrimony, Cloves, powder of Henbane. Beat all into a powder. Make thereof a paste with Foxes' blood and the brains of a Magpie.

CHARACTER OF OPHIEL LORD OF MERCURY

Perfumes:—

The seed of an Ash Tree, the wood of the Aloe, leaves of the Scullcap Herb, Mandrake roots, and the end of a Quill, made into small balls (pills).

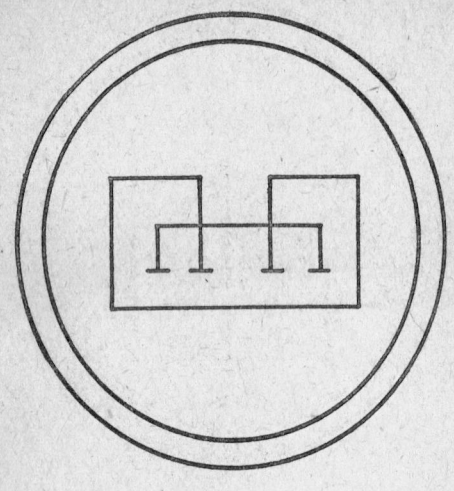

CHARACTER OF HAGITH LORD OF VENUS

Perfumes:—

Musk, Juniper berries, wood of Aloes, dried Red Roses, dried leaves of Elder, pulverized, and made into a paste with the blood of a Pigeon.

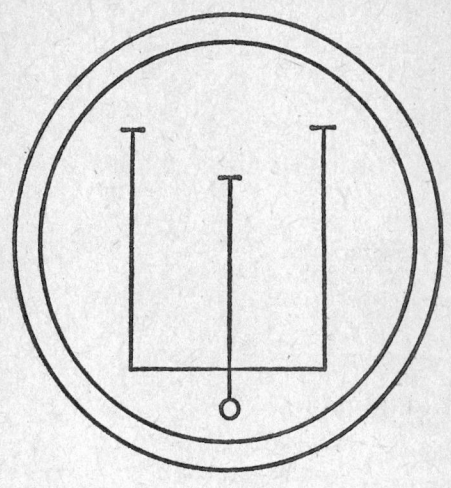

CHARACTER OF OCH LORD OF THE SUN

Perfumes:—

Grains of Black Pepper, grains of Hogsbane, powder of Sulphur, made into a paste with the blood of a Bat, and the brains of a black Cat.

Part the Second

Containing Invocations, Conjurations, and Exorcisms of the Band of Spirits

Form of Conjuring and Exorcising Spirits to Appear

Oration to be said when putting on the Vestures:—

Amacor, Amacor, Amides, Theodomai, Aintor, by the merits of Thy Angels, O Lord, I will put on the garments of Righteousness, that this which I desire I may bring to perfection through the most holy Adonay, Whose kingdom endureth for ever and ever. Amen.

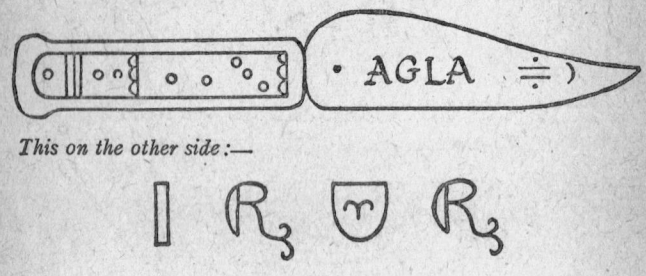

This on the other side :—

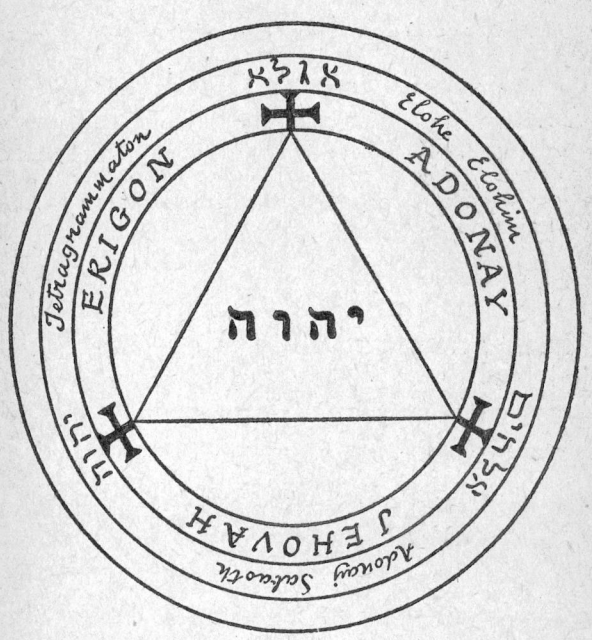

Prayer:—

O Holy, Holy Lord God, from Whom all holy desires do proceed, I beg Thou wilt be merciful unto me at this time, granting I may become a True Magician and contemplate of Thy wondrous works at all times, in the Name of the Father and of the Son. Therefore in all my doings and at all times I will call upon Thy Most Holy Name, O Lord, for Thy help and assistance.

I beseech Thee, O Lord, that Thou wilt purge me and wash me in the blood of our Saviour, from all my sins and frailties, and that Thou wilt henceforward vouchsafe to keep and defend me from pride, lusts, cursing, blasphemy, unfaithfulness, and all other deadly sins and enormous offences, profaneness and spiritual wickedness; but that I may lead a godly, sober, faithful, constant and pure life, walking uprightly in Thy sight, through the merits of Jesus Christ, Thy Son, our Lord and Saviour.

Omnipotent and Eternal Lord God Who sittest in Heaven and dost from thence behold all the dwellers upon earth, most mercifully I beseech Thee to hear and answer the petition of Thine unworthy servant, which I shall make unto Thee at this time, through Jesus Christ our Lord, Who liveth and reigneth with Thee in the unity of Thy Holy Spirit, ever One God, world without end.

Send down, O Lord, the Spirit of Thy Grace upon me. O God, put fear far from me, and give me an abundance of Thy Grace, and faith, whereby all things are made possible unto man; put every wicked phantom far from my mind, and grant me true zeal, fervour, and intentive spirit of zeal, and prayer, that I may offer up a well-pleasing sacrifice unto Thee. Let me use Thy ministering spirits and angels, O Lord, as thereby I may attain true wisdom and knowledge.

Our Father, etc.

Credo, etc.

Ave Maria, etc.

Glory be to the Father, Son, and Holy Ghost; as it was in the beginning, is now, and ever shall be, world without end. Amen.

Holy, Holy, Holy, Lord God of Sabaoth, which will come to judge the quick and the dead; Thou art Alpha and Omega, the first and the last, King of Kings, and Lord of

Lords, Ioth, Abiel, Anathiel, Amasim, Alganabro, El, Sedomel, Gayes, Heli, Messias, Tolosm, Elias, Eschiros, Athanatos; by these Thy Holy Names, and all others, I do call upon Thee and beseech Thee, O Lord, by Thy Nativity and baptism, by Thy Cross and Passion, by Thine ascension, and by the coming of Thy Holy Ghost, by the bitterness of Thy Soul when it departed from Thy body; by Thine Angels, Archangels, prophets, patriarchs, and by all Thy Saints, and by all the Sacraments which are made in Thine honour, I do worship and beseech Thee, I bless and desire Thee, to accept these prayers and conjurations.

I implore Thee, O Holy Adonay, Amay, Horta, Vegadoro, Ysion, Ysesy, and by all Thy Holy Names, and by all Thine Angels, Archangels, and Powers, Dominations, and Virtues, and by Thy Name with which King Solomon did bind up the devils and shut them up, Ethrack, Evanher, Agla, Goth, Joth, Othie, Venock, Nabrat, and by all Thy Holy Names which are written in this book, and by the virtue of them all, that Thou enable me to congregate all Thy spirits, that they may give me true answers to all my demands.

O Great and Eternal Virtue of the Highest, which Thou disposest their being come to judgment, Viachem, Stimilomaton, Esphares, Tetragrammaton, Oboram, Cryon, Elijtion, Onela, Brassim, Aoym, Messias, Soter, Emanuel, Sabaoth, Adonay, I worship Thee. I implore Thee with all the strength of my mind that by Thee my present prayers, consecrations, and conjurations may be hallowed. In the Name of the most merciful God of Heaven and of Earth, of the Seas and of the Infernals, by Thine Omnipotent help may I perform this Work.

Helie, Helion, Esseju, Deus Eternis, Eloy, Clemens Deus, Sanctus Sabaoth, Deus Exercillum, Adonay, Deus Mirabilis, Jao, Verax, Ampheneton, Saday, Dominator, On, Fortissimus Deus, invest with Thy blessed help this Work begun of Thee, that it may be consummated by Thy mighty power. Amen.

Amoruli, Tametia, Latisten, Rabur, Tanetia, Latisten, Escha, Aloelin, Alpha et Omega, Leytse, Oraston, Adonay. Amen.

Names and Offices of the Spirits, Messengers, and intelligences of the Seven Planets:—

Spirits of the Sun.

Gabriel.
Vianathraba.
Corat.

Messengers of the Sun.

Burchat.
Suceratos.
Capabile.

Intelligences of the Sun.

Haludiel.
Machasiel.
Chassiel.

Spirits of the Moon.

Gabriel.
Gabrael.
Madios.

Messengers of the Moon.

Anael.
Pabael.
Ustael.

Intelligences of the Moon.

Uriel.
Naromiel.
Abuori.

Spirits of Saturn.

Samael.
Bachiel.
Astel.

Messengers of Saturn.

Sachiel.
Zoniel.
Hubaril.

Intelligences of Saturn.

Mael.
Orael.
Valnum.

Spirits of Jupiter.

    Setchiel.
    Chedusitaniel.
    Corael.

Messengers of Jupiter.

    Turiel. (See Secret Grimoire of Turiel.)
    Coniel.
    Babiel.

Intelligences of Jupiter.

    Kadiel.
    Maltiel.
    Huphatriel.
    Estael.

Spirits of Venus.

    Thamael.
    Tenariel.
    Arragon.

Messengers of Venus.

    Colzras.
    Peniel.
    Penael.

Intelligences of Venus.

    Penat.
    Thiel.
    Rael.
    Teriapel.

Spirits of Mercury.

    Mathlai.
    Tarmiel.
    Baraborat.

Messengers of Mercury.

    Raphael.
    Ramel.
    Doremiel.

Intelligences of Mercury.

Aiediat.
Modiat.
Sugmonos.
Sallales.

Presiding Spirits of Jupiter.

Sachiel.
Castiel.
Asasiel.

Presiding Spirits of Venus.

Anael.
Rachiel.
Sachiel.

Presiding Spirits of Mars.

Samael.
Satael.
Amabiel.

Presiding Spirits of Mercury.

Raphael.
Uriel.
Seraphiel.

O Angeli Glorioso supradicti estote coadjutores et auxi-
liatores in omnibus negotijs et interrogationibus in omnibus
celensq (?) causis per Eum qui venturus est judiciase vivos
et mortuos.

———

Omnipotent and Eternal God Who hast ordained the
whole creation for Thy praise and glory and for the salvation of man, I earnestly beseech Thee that Thou wouldst
send one of Thy spirits of the Order of Jupiter, one of the
messengers of Sachiel whom Thou hast appointed presiding
spirit of Thy firmament at this time, most faithfully, willingly to show unto me those things which I shall demand or
require of him, and truly execute my desires. Nevertheless,
O most Holy God, Thy will and not mine be done, through
Jesus Christ our Lord. Amen.

Invocation:—

I call upon thee, Sachiel, Castiel, and Asasiel, in the Name of the Father, and of the Son, and of the Holy Ghost, Blessed Trinity, Inseparable Unity, I invoke and entreat thee, Sachiel, Castiel, and Asasiel, in this hour to attend to the words and conjurations which I shall use by the Holy Names of God, El, Elohim, Elohe, Eeoba, Sabaoth, Elion, Eschiros, Adonay, Jay, Tetragrammaton, Saday; I conjure and excite you by the Holy Names of God, Hagios, Otheos, Ischyros, Athanatos, Paracletos, Agla, On, Alpha and Omega, Ausias, Tolimi, Elias, Imos, Amay, Horta, Vegadora, Antir, Sibranat, Amatha, Baldachia, Anuoram, Anexpheton, Via, Vita, Manus, Fons, Origo, Filius

and by all the other Holy, Glorious, Great, and Unspeakable, Mysterious, Mighty, Powerful, and Incomprehensible Names of God, that you attend unto the words which I shall utter, and send unto me Turiel, Coniel, or Babiel, messengers of your sphere, to tell unto me such things as I shall demand of him, in the Name of the Father, Son, and Holy Ghost.

I entreat thee, Setchiel, Chedustaniel, and Corael, by the whole host of Heaven, Seraphims, Cherubims, Thrones, Dominations, Virtues, Powers, Principalities, Archangels and Angels, by the great and glorious Spirits Orphaniel, Tetra, Pagiel, Salmia, Pastor, Salun, Azimor, and by your Star which is Jupiter, and by all the constellations of Heaven, and by whatsoever you obey, and by your Character which you have given and proposed and confirmed, that you attend unto me according to the prayers and petitions which I have made unto Almighty God, and that you forthwith send unto me one of your messengers who may willingly and truly and faithfully fulfil all my desires, wishes and commands, and that you command him to appear unto me in form of a beautiful angel clothed in white vestures, gently, courteously, kindly, and affably entering into communication with me, and that he neither bring terror nor fear unto me, or obstinately deny my requests, neither permitting any evil spirits to appear or approach in any way to hurt, terrify, or affright me, nor deceiving me in any wise; through the virtue of our Lord and Saviour Jesus Christ, in Whose Name I attend, waiting for and expecting your appearance. Fiat, Fiat, Fiat.   Amen.

Interrogations:—

'Comest thou in peace, in the Name of the Father, and of the Son, and of the Holy Ghost?'
'Yes.'
'Thou art welcome, noble Spirit. What is thy name?'
'Turiel.'
'I have called thee here, Turiel, in the Name of Jesus of Nazareth, at Whose Name every knee doth bow, both of things in Heaven, Earth, and Hell, and every tongue shall confess there is no Name like unto the Name of Jesus, Who hath given power unto man to bind and to loose all things in His Name, yea, even unto them that trust in His salvation. Art thou the messenger of Setchiel?'
'Yes.'
'Wilt thou confirm thyself unto me at this time, and from henceforward reveal all things unto me that I shall desire to know and teach me how to increase my wisdom and knowledge, and show unto me the secrets of the Magick Art, and of the liberal sciences, that I may set forth the praise and glory of Almighty God?'
'Yes.'
'Then, I pray thee, give and confirm thy Character unto me, whereby I may call thee at all times, and also swear unto me this Oath, and I will religiously keep my vow and covenant unto Almighty God, and will courteously receive thee at all times when thou dost appear to me.'

Licence to Depart:—

'Forasmuch as thou camest in peace and quietness and hast answered me and unto my petitions, I give humble and hearty thanks unto Almighty God, in whose Name I called thee and thou camest. And now thou mayest depart in peace unto thy Orders, and return unto me again at what time soever I shall call thee by thine own Oath, or by thy name, or by thine Order, or by thine Office which is granted from the Creator. And the Grace of God be with thee and me and upon the whole Israel of God. Amen. Glory be to the Father, and to the Son, and to the Holy Ghost, as it was in the beginning, is now, and ever shall be, world without end. Fiat. Fiat. Fiat. Amen.'

Form of a Bond of Spirits given by Turiel, Messenger of the Spirits of Jupiter:—

Gloria Deo in Excelsis.

I, Turiel, Messenger of the Spirits of Jupiter, appointed thereunto by the Creator of all things visible and invisible, do swear and promise, and plighting faith and troth unto thee in the presence, by, and before the Great Lord of Heaven

and the whole company of Heaven, by all the Holy Names of God, do swear and bind myself unto thee, by all the contents of God's Sacred Writ, by the Incarnation, death and passion, resurrection, and glorious Ascension of Jesus Christ, by all the Holy Sacraments, by the Mercy of God, by the Glory and Eyes of Heaven, by the forgiveness of sin, and hope of eternal salvation, by the Great Day of Doom, by all the Angels and Archangels, Seraphim, Cherubim, Dominations, Thrones, Principalities, Powers, and Virtues, Patriarchs, Prophets, Saints, Martyrs, Innocents, and all others of the blessed and glorious Company of Heaven, and by all the sacred powers and virtues above rehearsed, and by whatever is holy and binding, thus do I swear now, and promise unto thee that I will hasten unto thee, and appear clearly unto thee at all times and places, and in all hours, days, and minutes, from this time forward until thy life's end, whensoever thou shalt call me by my name, or by my Office, and will come unto thee in what form thou shalt desire, whether it be visibly or invisibly; I will answer all thy desires. And in testimony whereof, and before all the Powers of Heaven, I have hereunto set, subscribed, and confirmed my Character unto thee.

So help me God.   Fiat.   Amen.

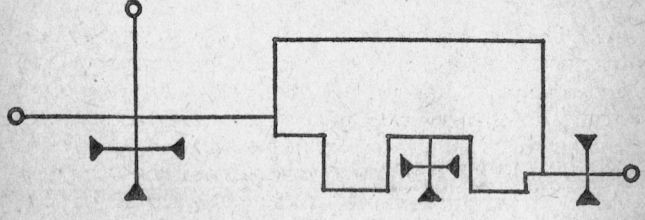

The Character of Turiel

FINIS

The Powers and Offices of the Seven Olympic Spirits are as follows :—

ARATRON governs those things which are ascribed astrologically to Saturn. He can convert any living organism, plant or animal into stone, and that in a moment of time; he can also change coals into treasure and treasure into coals; he gives familiars and reconciles subterranean spirits to men; he teaches alchemy, magick, and medicine, imparts the secret of invisibility, makes the barren fruitful, and lastly, confers long life. He should be invoked on a Saturday, in the first hour of the day, making use of his Character, given and confirmed by himself.

The affairs of Jupiter are administered by BETHOR, who responds quickly when called. The person dignified by his Character will be exalted to illustrious positions, and may obtain large treasures. He reconciles the spirits of the air to man, so that they will give true answers, transport precious stones, and compose medicines having miraculous effects. Bethor also grants familiars of the firmament, and can prolong life to the True Magician, subject always to the fervour and purity of the latter.

PHALEG governs the things that are attributed to Mars. The person who possesses his Character is raised by him to great honour in military affairs and business concerns.

Solar interests are administered by OCH, who prolongs life to the True Magician, with perfect health therein. He imparts great wisdom, gives excellent familiar spirits, composes perfect medicines, converts any substance into the purest of metals, or into precious stones; he also bestows gold, and a purse springing with gold. He causes the possessor of his Character to be worshipped as a god by the kings of the whole world.

The government of Venereal concerns (i.e. those of Venus) is entrusted to HAGITH, and the person possessing his Character is adorned with all beauty. He converts copper into gold in a moment, and gold instantaneously into copper; he also gives faithful serving spirits.

OPHIEL is the ruler of those things which are attributed to Mercury; he gives familiar spirits, teaches all arts, and enables the possessor of his Character to change quicksilver immediately into the Philosophers' Stone.

Lunary concerns (i.e. those of the Moon) are under the government of PHUL, who truly transmutes all metals into silver, heals dropsy, and provides spirits of the water who serve men in a corporal and visible body, and prolongs the life of the True Magician.

Legions of inferior spirits are commanded by each of the Governors, who also have Kings, Princes, Presidents, Dukes, and Ministers ruling under them. Ceremonial Magick usually administers the hierarchies upon a colossal scale. The invocation of the Governors is simple. It is performed in the day and hour of the planet which is in correspondence with the Olympic Intelligence by means of the following Prayer :—

'O Eternal and Omnipotent God, Who hast ordained the whole creation for Thy praise and Thy glory, as also for the salvation of man, I beseech Thee, send Thy spirit (Name) of the Solar Race (1),* that he may instruct me concerning those things about which I design to ask him (or, that he may bring me medicine against the dropsy, etc.). Nevertheless, not my will but Thine be done, through our Lord Jesus Christ, Thine Only Begotten Son.   Amen.'

The Lords of the Planets (according to the Ancient Grimoires):—

SATURN : ARATRON.
MARS : PHALEG.
MOON : PHUL.
JUPITER : BETHOR.
MERCURY : OPHIEL.
VENUS : HAGITH.
SUN : OCH.

See the Chart of the Planetary Hours for evocation of spirits of the various planets.

*(1). This is merely a typical form, subject, of course, to variations according to the spirit who is evoked.

Time of Planetary Hours Computed from Midnight to Midnight.

Hours of the Day

	Sunday	Monday	Tuesday	Wednesday	Thursday	Friday	Saturday
1	Sun	Moon	Mars	Mercury	Jupiter	Venus	Saturn
2	Venus	Saturn	Sun	Moon	Mars	Mercury	Jupiter
3	Mercury	Jupiter	Venus	Saturn	Sun	Moon	Mars
4	Moon	Mars	Mercury	Jupiter	Venus	Saturn	Sun
5	Saturn	Sun	Moon	Mars	Mercury	Jupiter	Venus
6	Jupiter	Venus	Saturn	Sun	Moon	Mars	Mercury
7	Mars	Mercury	Jupiter	Venus	Saturn	Sun	Moon
8	Sun	Moon	Mars	Mercury	Jupiter	Venus	Saturn
9	Venus	Saturn	Sun	Moon	Mars	Mercury	Jupiter
10	Mercury	Jupiter	Venus	Saturn	Sun	Moon	Mars
11	Moon	Mars	Mercury	Jupiter	Venus	Saturn	Sun
12	Saturn	Sun	Moon	Mars	Mercury	Jupiter	Venus

Hours of the Night

	Sunday	Monday	Tuesday	Wednesday	Thursday	Friday	Saturday
1	Jupiter	Venus	Saturn	Sun	Moon	Mars	Mercury
2	Mars	Mercury	Jupiter	Venus	Saturn	Sun	Moon
3	Sun	Moon	Mars	Mercury	Jupiter	Venus	Saturn
4	Venus	Saturn	Sun	Moon	Mars	Mercury	Jupiter
5	Mercury	Jupiter	Venus	Saturn	Sun	Moon	Mars
6	Moon	Mars	Mercury	Jupiter	Venus	Saturn	Sun
7	Saturn	Sun	Moon	Mars	Mercury	Jupiter	Venus
8	Jupiter	Venus	Saturn	Sun	Moon	Mars	Mercury
9	Mars	Mercury	Jupiter	Venus	Saturn	Sun	Moon
10	Sun	Moon	Mars	Mercury	Jupiter	Venus	Saturn
11	Venus	Saturn	Sun	Moon	Mars	Mercury	Jupiter
12	Mercury	Jupiter	Venus	Saturn	Sun	Moon	Mars

The Dennis Wheatley Library of the Occult

In this paperback series we propose to include novels and uncanny tales by:

Marjorie Bowen, John Buchan, Ambrose Bierce, R. H. and E. F. Benson, Brodie-Innes, Balzac, Algernon Blackwood, F. Marion Crawford, Wilkie Collins, Aleister Crowley, Dickens, Conan-Doyle, Dostoyevsky, Lord Dunsany, Guy Endore, Dion Fortune, Kipling, Le Fanu, Bulwer Lytton, Walter de la Mare, A. E. W. Mason, Arthur Machen, John Masefield, Guy de Maupassant, Oliver Onions, Edgar Alan Poe, Sax Rohmer, Bram Stoker, W. B. Seabrook, H. G. Wells, Hugh Walpole and Oscar Wilde.

Aslo books on:

Palmistry, Astrology, Faith Healing, Clairvoyance, Numerology, Telepathy, etc.

For particulars write to Sphere Books Ltd, 30/32 Gray's Inn Road, London WC1X 8JL.

All Sphere Books are available at your bookshop or
newsagent, or can be ordered from the following address:

Sphere Books, Cash Sales Department,
P.O. Box 11, Falmouth, Cornwall.

Please send cheque or postal order (no currency), and allow
7p per copy to cover the cost of postage and packing
in U.K., or overseas.